"Floy Turner and Sherrie Clark's latest book BEHIND HER CRIMINAL INVESTIGATOR'S BADGE is a definite must read." I started reading it and couldn't put it down until I finished it. Then I read it again. Every time a new case started, I followed the twists and turns of the clues and leads until the case was resolved. And as a former FBI Agent assigned to Miami, it brought back memories of my experiences after 9-11, kidnapping cases I had worked, etc.

"The book is especially good at highlighting the roller-coaster ride of emotions that an investigator experiences while working a case. It can range from concern that the initial leads are sparse. Then as leads develop, the excitement builds, and finally a sigh of relief when the case is solved and the bad guy is behind bars. The successful recovery of a kidnapped child is the best feeling and being unable to save a child is the worst feeling. All of these emotions are woven into the cases in the book.

"I applaud Floy Turner's long service in law enforcement, and her ability to share her experiences in this book."

VICKI MELLON
Special Agent (Retired)
Federal Bureau of Investigation (FBI)

"BEHIND HER CRIMINAL INVESTIGATOR'S BADGE by Floy Turner and Sherrie Clark is an unforgettable read. From 9/11, serial killers, murderous mothers, child pornographers, sexual predators and human trafficking, the intensity never lets up. My emotions took a complete rollercoaster ride on this, their third book. Floy lays it all out in this book and the least I can say is that I am in awe of all she accomplished and gave to the citizens of Florida. Don't skip one page of this amazing book."

TRISH ENGLAND
State Trooper, Retired
Florida Highway Patrol

"Floy Turner and Sherrie Clark's latest endeavor is by far the most poignant, heartfelt, and informative. A true accounting of what our children and adults face in the world when it comes to protecting children. Absolutely a 'must-read'"!

ALAN P. WOLOCHUK
Chief (Retired)
California Highway Patrol

"Reader beware. Once you begin to read *Behind Her Criminal Investigator's Badge*, you will not be able to put it down. Building on her previous two books covering earlier parts of her storied career, Floy Turner now allows us to come along as she investigates a full range of complex, high-profile criminal cases. You have the unique opportunity to understand what really happens with the different type of cases through the eyes of an accomplished, acclaimed investigator.

"Floy shares her passion for working missing children cases and developing the Child Abduction Response Team concept and shines a light on working domestic minor sex trafficking cases. Enjoy this exceptional book and make sure to read Floy Turner and Sherrie Clark's earlier works as well — *Behind Her Miami Badge* and *Behind Her Special Agent Badge*."

BILL KEARNEY
Owner, WBKEARNEY & Associates

"Floy has been investigating human trafficking cases before a law even existed. Her knowledge and experience in investigating human trafficking cases is bar none. It's been an honor working with Floy."

ANNA RODRIQUEZ
Author of Ma'am Anna: The Remarkable Story of a Human
    Trafficking Rescuer
Founder & Executive Director,
Florida Coalition Against Human Trafficking

"Behind Her Criminal Investigator's Badge is a beautifully written book that provides an illuminating, interesting, and heartwarming glimpse into the heart and soul of a warrior working behind the thin blue line. Sherrie Clark skillfully captures the passion and dedication of Floy Turner as she pits her wits and experience against perverts and pedophiles who prey on the innocence of our youngsters. The reader of this book will gain a new appreciation for the men and women who spend their lives combating evil and keeping us safe."

SHIRLEY SHAW
Editor-in-Chief (Retired)
Victims' Advocate award-winning newspaper

"If you want a book that possesses both fast-paced action and a poignant story, BEHIND HER SPECIAL AGENT BADGE will not disappoint. Not only will you be able to experience crime fighting firsthand, but Turner and Clark take you on exhilarating ride one moment and then give you an emotional punch the next."

SUSAN AMBROSINO
Police Officer
NYPD, Transit D-32

"Another provocative peek behind the scenes of law enforcement from the perspective of a tough but compassionate female investigator. Witty and insightful, sad and shocking."

JILLIANE HOFFMAN
Best-Selling Author

"Clark and Turner hit the ball out of the park with their last book in this trilogy. This is the real deal of law enforcement…the truth and nothing but the truth. Spectacular!"

JANE DOUGHERTY
Police Officer (Retired)
NYPD

"The reader has the rare opportunity to "ride along" with America's law enforcement heroes in the aftermath of 9/11 and experience the battle against human traffickers from the safety of their own living room. A riveting, fascinating read!"

GARY MARTIN HAYS
Attorney, Best-Selling Author
TV and Radio Show Host
Board Member, Elizabeth Smart Foundation

"BEHIND HER CRIMINAL INVESTIGATOR'S BADGE is a wonderfully written account of Turner's amazing career. It delves into some of the darkest cases and people that a law enforcement officer encounters but also the human, emotional side, emotions that are real but must be shelved to get the job done. This book offers true insight into this often-misunderstood profession and of those who dedicate their lives to making their communities a safer place for everyone. For those who have done the job, are considering it, or someone who wants to better understand it, this book is a must read!"

DONNA BROWN
Homicide Detective Sergeant (Retired)
Tallahassee Police Department

"For those who are interested in police work, this is a must-read before plunging into the special and elite club of law enforcement. You'll learn the good, the bad, and the ugly of wearing a badge as Turner and Clark make you feel as if you're there, experiencing it yourself. Absolutely riveting!"

ANN TOWPASH
Lieutenant (Retired)
NYPD

BEHIND HER CRIMINAL INVESTIGATOR'S BADGE

*9/11, Missing and Exploited Children,
and Life in the Pursuit of Human Traffickers*

Floy Turner

&

Sherrie Clark

BEHIND HER CRIMINAL INVESTIGATOR'S BADGE: 9/11, Missing and Exploited Children, and Life in the Pursuit of Human Traffickers

Storehouse Media Group, LLC
Jacksonville, Florida
www.StorehouseMediaGroup.com
Hello@StorehouseMediaGroup.com

Ordering Information:

Quantity sales. Special discounts are available with the Publisher at the email address above and type in subject line "Special Sales Department."

Cover Photo by Renee Tyler

BEHIND HER CRIMINAL INVESTIGATOR'S BADGE / Floy Turner and Sherrie Clark —1st ed.

ISBN: 978-1-943106-36-3 (paperback)
ISBN: 978-1-943106-37-0 (ebook)

Library of Congress Control Number: 2018945551

Printed in the United States of America

DEDICATION

I want to dedicate this book to the memory of Kellie Carmichael Thomas, a loving daughter and wife to Chris and mother to three beautiful young children

I also want to dedicate this book to my husband, Gary Carmichael, who I dearly love and to our family Kally, Reg and Mary Ellen, and Scott and our sweet grandchildren.

FLOY TURNER

I also want to dedicate this book to my family: Darryl, Devlin, Tristan, Liam, Micah, Janna, and Buddy, Gracie, and Chloe.

SHERRIE CLARK

We also want to dedicate this book to the heroes from 9/11 and to the heroes who have and are still giving their all since.

FLOY TURNER and **SHERRIE CLARK**

EPIGRAPH

"*Rescue the weak and the needy; deliver them from the hand of the wicked.*"
Psalm 82:4 (NIV)

DISCLAIMER

The purpose of this book is to entertain while enlightening readers to certain events from 2001 onward from the perspective of state law enforcement officer Floy Turner. It's based on actual events that occurred during the last years of her tenure as a Special Agent with the Florida Department of Law Enforcement. Turner has made every effort to recreate events, places, and conversations as accurately as possible from her memories of them as well as through research.

Turner's immediate family gave her permission to use their real names. Also, the actual names of those who have been written about in the news have been used. To protect the privacy and anonymity of everyone else involved in this book, she has changed their names, the names of places, and any identifying characteristics and details, and she has modified some of the circumstances. Any similarities to anyone you think you may know are coincidental.

This book does include a few words that some may find offensive. They are written as they had been spoken so that the stories retain their authenticity.

The authors and publisher shall have neither liability nor responsibility to any person or entity with respect to any loss or damage caused, or alleged to have been caused, directly or indirectly, or disruptions caused by errors or omissions, whether such errors or omissions result from negligence, accident, or any other cause, by the information contained in this book.

CONTENTS

PREFACE

FLOY TURNER:

When Sherrie Clark and I first met, we were both involved with the North East Florida Human Trafficking Coalition. Later, Sherrie who served at the time as a reporter, covered a mock child abduction exercise that I had created and utilized for Child Abduction Response Team outside of Atlanta, Georgia. We instantly felt a bond since Sherrie had served as a police officer with New York City Police Department.

Sherrie approached me inquiring if I would write a book about my twenty-five years as a law enforcement officer with the State of Florida. Little did I know, when I gave her the go ahead with this project that it would turn into three books! My journey as an author fortunately was guided by a professional who is the best wordsmith I can imagine. Sherrie taught me the ins and outs of writing, and as my story came to life. I was thrilled with the final outcome of the *Badges* series.

The best part of my journey has been hearing from our readers who truly enjoyed our books. Sherrie and I have become partners and the best of friends. We share a love of God, family and friends and country. God blessed me with the opportunity to serve as a guardian for justice and peace.

SHERRIE CLARK:

Writing and crafting the *Badges* series for the past five years has been a beyond-fun adventure for me. Of course, I couldn't have asked for a better partner. I have grown to know Floy Turner, and I am still in awe at her courage and accomplishments. Truly, what you read about her is what you get.

From the first email she sent for the writing of our first book BEHIND HER MIAMI BADGE to the final word written in its final book, BEHIND HER CRIMINAL INVESTIGATOR'S BADGE, the journey has been exciting. I truly enjoyed describing the scenes I would see in my head as Floy shared her life and investigations and how she saved another child. The scenes involved a myriad of emotions within me, some of which I may never have experienced if not for writing this series.

Working and completing this last book in the BADGES series has been bittersweet, though. I'm excited that you will be able to read the remainder of Floy's career in law enforcement; that's the sweet part. On the other hand, I have found nearing the end to be a bit sad, knowing that that part of my writing life is nearing the end as well. That's the bitter part. Regardless, I will always have Floy's friendship, and I will always enjoy the comments and feedback from you, the reader. Writing this series has given me the privilege and honor of experiencing both.

As you read Floy's final stories as a Florida Department of Law Enforcement Special Agent, I am again confident that you'll deepen your admiration of her besides, in front or, and behind the badge!

ACKNOWLEDGMENTS

Thank you to everyone who has joined us in our journey of writing this book series. Some of you have been with us the whole way while some have been with us for a season. Regardless, every one of you has given to our efforts in unique ways that have been greatly appreciated and all has contributed to our series' success.

We want to give a special thanks to our proofreaders who applied their skills to our BADGES series: Shirley Shaw, Patrick Hodges, Sandy Sledge, and Vicki Mellon. You did a great job.

So many of you supported us, before, during, after, and in between the writing and publishing of our books. Your word-of-mouth and written reviews were so much appreciated. Although we would love to name names, but that would take pages upon pages. You know who you are, so we give you our deepest thanks.

Also, thank you to Devlin Kidney for creating our book trailers. You've captured the essence of the stories wonderfully.

Thank you to Lee Ann Howlett for being our voice and narrating BEHIND HER MIAMI BADGE'S and BEHIND HER SPECIAL AGENT'S BADGE'S audiobooks. You did a wonderful job.

And a big thanks to all our readers!

__FLOY TURNER:__

First, I want to thank my husband who is always my biggest fan. I was so fortunate to be assigned to his squad during Hurricane Opal. I love you, Gary. I also want to thank my family Kally, Reg and Mary Ellen and Scott.

Thanks to the PLOCK Book Club members who have embraced my books and offered me support throughout my writing process. All of you are dear friends.

Another thank you to the Ruth Circle members from First Presbyterian Church of Vero Beach who have kept me uplifted through our shared fellowship.

To the Ashland, Kentucky Super Beachbuds: Sallie Alexander, Kathy Jerrell, Malinda Coleman, Peggy Thirion, Peggy Calhoun, Jetta Wright, Nancy Alia, Barby Faris, Melaine Frank, Nagatha Kendrick, Cissy Blevins, Cheryl Townsend, Connie Waespe, Gale Barton, and Cherie Schofield who have shown so much love through fun times and communication thanks for the memories and new times.

Sherrie Clark has been with me though out the "Badges" books. Without her encouragement and vision, my story would not have been told. Thanks, Sherrie.

<u>SHERRIE CLARK:</u>

I always love to give thanks to my family Darryl Clark, Devlin Kidney, Tristan Kidney, Liam Kidney, Micah Clark, and Janna Clark, for all of your support, encouragement, and yes, patience with my writing ventures. Knowing you have my back motivates me in my endeavors.

I want to thank Rhonda Biondi, Marsha Geoghagan, Fran Futril, Audrey Kendrick, Debbie Dykes, Annie Towpash, Sue Kinzie, Dr. Michele Fleming, Lois Kidney, and Richard Kidney for your friendship and feedback on this book and other *Badges* books.

I want to thank Floy Turner, for giving me the honor and privilege to craft and develop your stories. Your confidence in my abilities have encouraged me, and your friendship has enriched my life, both professionally and personally.

CHAPTER ONE

9/11 – A DAY NEVER TO BE FORGOTTEN

September 11, 2001. A day that started like every other day, yet a day no one would ever forget.

I enjoyed my run that Tuesday morning, speeding along my route with great zeal. I welcomed the solitude, using this time to think through my cases, to strategize, and to pray.

I couldn't stop thinking about one of my last cases, which continued to have a profound impact on me professionally as well as personally. To me, when a child is murdered, it's unacceptable that he or she doesn't get justice. Little Nancy Goodyear was only five when her life came to a tragic and nonsensical end. What made it worse was knowing beyond a shadow of a doubt the identity of her murderer. Try as we might, we could never get him to confess. I replayed the case over and over in my mind, hoping to find something, even the minutest detail we might have overlooked.

Taking full advantage of my environment, I shifted my thoughts to something more pleasant and positive. I allowed my eyes to take in the beautiful, clear sky, my nostrils to smell the sea salt dispersed throughout the atmosphere, and my skin to feel the light ocean breeze that acted as a low-powered fan. Still, it wasn't enough to alleviate the internal heat created by my intense run. By the time I entered my home, I was dripping with sweat.

Coffee had brewed during my run, and its aroma beckoned me. Normally, I appreciated a quiet house, but I missed my husband Gary.

On Sunday, he and six other FDLE (Florida Department of Law Enforcement) Special Agents had flown up to the Federal Law Enforcement Training Center (FLETC) in Glencoe, Georgia, to attend a five-day Seaport Security training class. I looked forward to his return at the end of the week.

Out the back door, I noticed that my Rottweiler Hardy and rescued dog Little Bit were ready to come inside after their outdoor time on the patio. I let them back into the house while I finished drinking my coffee.

Little Bit made herself comfortable by stretching out on her bed. She had only been with us a short time. I smiled as I remembered how only a few months earlier, this black-and-tan puppy came out of the woods during my morning run. She followed me for the remaining mile, all the way to my house.

Her eyes had been infected, and she had sores on her skin. Poor thing… probably dumped by some irresponsible jerk, leaving this puppy to fend for herself. She looked like she hadn't eaten in weeks, her ribs protruding through her dull coat. I gave her food and water before dropping her off at the vet on my way to work.

When I picked her up that afternoon, my efforts had earned me an expensive vet bill. I considered her to be an investment, so Gary and I adopted her and named her Little Bit. She had been a part of our family ever since.

After a quick shower, I selected a dark suit to wear for work. The *Today Show* played on my bedroom's television while I dressed.

I sat on the edge of my bed and bent over to put on my shoes. My mind focused on what I had planned for the day and paid little attention to the television playing in front of me.

An announcement interrupted the show, and thus my thoughts, informing viewers that a plane had just crashed into the upper part of the World Trade Center's North Tower in New York City. My head jerked up, and my eyes became glued to the replay of the crash footage.

My breathing quickened as I tried to make sense of the sight on my screen. Before I made any progress, I saw a second plane strike the South Tower of the World Trade Center. I immediately knew the United States was under a terrorist attack.

My police training kicked into high gear. I changed out of my suit and into tactical police attire. I grabbed my phone and called the office. My staff assistant answered on the fourth ring. "Is the television on there?" I asked.

"Yes. Everyone is in the conference room watching these horrible things happening."

Keeping my eyes glued on the screen, I said, "I'm going to be watching from my house until I hear any further news."

Then I hung up, realizing afterward I hadn't even said goodbye. I began to make a mental assessment of the provisions I already had in my car. I wanted to top off my gas tank, just in case.

Even being so far away from the initial attacks, I realized Florida could be the target of future attacks. I still needed to be prepared due to my obligation to protect and serve as a Special Agent with the FDLE. This included working with other agencies in strengthening our domestic security.

Gary called me from Georgia. We talked about the World Trade Center incident without going into detail over the phone.

He then said, "Floy, the rest of our training class was just canceled. I'm trying to get a flight back home as soon as possible."

We quickly learned that all commercial aircraft were grounded until further notice. Gary called to let me know he was trying to rent a car to drive home.

With the entire commercial airline fleet sitting idle, I recognized that this catastrophic event had caught the United States unprepared. As a result, thousands of passengers, their luggage, and a huge number of cargo planes ended up not being able to move for days and days.

I took a moment to call my daughters.

Just as I finished talking to my youngest daughter, the television announced that another plane had just crashed into the Pentagon. My heart skipped a beat, and my throat went dry. I fought to keep my emotions at bay. That was my human side. The cop in me had questions, suspicions, and lots of frustration from not being able to do anything to stop whatever was coming next.

At that moment, I could only try to protect my loved ones. I called my mother, who lived less than a mile from our Boynton Beach home.

When she answered, she sounded out of breath. My level of concern raised even higher.

"Mom, you okay? What's going on?"

"Oh, Floy, after seeing the attacks on TV, I just wanted to get away from the sight, and so I tripped over my cat and fell. I think I may have broken my wrist."

Now my concern level went through the roof. I left immediately to help her.

I worried about my mom. Before meeting my father, she had been married to an Army Air Corps pilot. During World War II, he had been shot down over North Africa and died. I think the attack on our soil brought back a lot of those memories and thus startled her so much that she became breathless and tripped over the cat.

After picking her up, I took her to an urgent care clinic. I walked into the light-colored reception area wearing my tactical gear, FDLE shirt, badge, and gun. No one noticed me. All of those waiting to see a doctor as well as some of the staff were mesmerized by the surreal images playing on the television in the waiting room. I watched from the corner of my eye before stopping to witness the South Tower collapse. The moans and cries erupting from the small room confirmed my own feelings.

My mind raced with the possibility of more attacks, yet my first concern was my mom. She needed to be taken care of before I could do anything else. Tending to her would take some time, so I called my office to inform them of my whereabouts.

As soon as I hung up, the news reported that another plane, United Airlines Flight 93, went down in Pennsylvania. I instantly knew all of these crashes were connected. Sitting idle in the waiting room caused me to feel like a caged animal, eager and obligated to get out there and do *something*. Then about twenty minutes later, I watched the North Tower collapse.

My attire clearly identified me as a law enforcement officer, so I told the medical staff that I may be called into work. I asked if they could expedite my mother. I hated to jump line, but our country was being attacked. This would affect many, many lives, and I knew I would be needed.

The receptionist gave a single nod. In a hoarse voice, she said, "Yes, officer. Be assured we'll work with you to get your mother taken care of as soon as possible so that you can do your job."

She kept her word. The staff surpassed what seemed to be all-time records in getting Mom into X-ray. After the doctor confirmed that she had a break in her right wrist, he quickly put a cast on it and wrote the needed prescriptions.

Relieved to get Mom's problem addressed, I helped her into my car. We stopped at the pharmacy to fill her prescriptions. I then took her back to her condominium, got her settled in, and informed her neighbor. She promised to check in on her.

Just as I climbed into my car, Gary called again. His tone was serious, which was understandable.

"I just talked to my dad. He's been watching this morning's events, and he's crying uncontrollably."

Gary's dad was eighteen years old when the Japanese attacked Pearl Harbor in 1941. Like so many other young boys, Mr. Carmichael had immediately joined the U.S. Armed Forces, vowing revenge for that sneak attack. His desire for justice led to his fighting in World War II and Korea. He retired as a U.S. Army Master Sergeant.

I figured that he, like Mom, was experiencing some negative flashbacks.

Searching the Terrorists' Condos

I went back home to finish more needed preparations just in case I got deployed.

By early afternoon, the FDLE office contacted me. They told me to head to the Miami FBI Office for a four o'clock meeting.

Finally, I could spend some of this pent-up energy and do something for my country. I placed extra dog food and water on the back porch next to the doggy door. Normally, I'd keep the dogs inside while I was gone. With Gary out of town, though, I didn't want to worry about them needing to go outside to take care of business.

I began the hour-long drive to Miami. After exiting off I-95 at the Golden Glades Interchange, I drove a few blocks before reaching the dismal and drab concrete building that housed the FBI.

I always wondered why this building looked outdated, even while it was being built. I found it ugly both on the inside and the outside. Furthermore, the utilitarian design gave no thought to décor, making the structure feel cold.

My mind reverted back to the plane crashes. All those innocent passengers had started their day just like everyone else, but now they had no more days. Like most Americans, I felt apprehensive not knowing if there were any more attacks coming, and if so, when… and where? My body tensed up like a boxer preparing herself for the next punch.

I was on autopilot as I walked through the shabby-looking, bland courtyard to the lower level of the building. A blue-uniformed security guard manned a checkpoint and metal detector. I showed him my credentials, and he ushered me inside.

The elevator took me to the second floor where I joined about a hundred FDLE and FBI agents in a large, gray room with rows of brown-tweed chairs covering thin, gray carpet. I saw a lot of familiar faces, but most seemed engaged in conversations, speaking in hushed tones. Others looked stunned, sitting or standing and staring at nothing in particular or down at the ground.

I sat in an empty chair, glad to be alone with my thoughts. A door next to a large conference room kept opening and closing as FDLE and FBI supervisors entered and left. Each time the door opened, I could see supervisors and phone banks surrounding a massive conference table.

A familiar face walked into the room. It belonged to FBI Special Agent Karen Kool. We had become close when we worked together on little Nancy Goodyear's cold case murder. Her furrowed brows, unfocused eyes, and downturned mouth made her seem preoccupied.

When she saw me, though, her face lit up. Her genuine smile always had a way of making her blue eyes twinkle. Her short brown hair had grown a little longer, but her ruddy complexion remained.

She walked over and hugged me, both as a greeting and for comfort. We spoke for a few minutes.

"Supervisors are putting together teams," Karen said. "I hope we'll be working together."

"What are the teams going to be investigating?" I asked.

Her smile disappeared. "Seven or more of the hijackers lived in South Florida. Assignments are being organized to gather information about their activities."

My head spun upon learning about the connection between South Florida and the 9/11 hijackers. Before this information could sink in, one of the FBI supervisors came out of that conference room. Everyone grew quiet as we eagerly awaited any announcement he may deliver.

He complied. "The FBI has information linking many of the possible hijackers to our area. I'll be calling out the names of agents to partner together for this detail. Some of the teams will be responding to known places where these hijackers lived."

He went on to explain that the terrorists had been identified thanks to two brave flight attendants on American Airlines Flight 11. These heroes had called American Airlines from the plane and gave the hijackers' seat numbers.

The feds were then able to obtain Mohamed Atta's identity from the credit card information. We later learned through the investigation that he was believed to be one of the ringleaders and to have piloted Flight 11 as it struck the North Tower.

For the time being, though, investigators had discovered that Atta lived at the Racket Club in Delray Beach. To know these monsters lived in our communities and then killed thousands of innocent Americans in just a few short hours appalled me.

Reading off the clipboard, the supervisor called out assignments. I was to work with two fairly new FBI agents, but not Karen. Although disappointed, I was admittedly curious about my new partners. Both of them had been with the Bureau for about a year, but I was sure their experiences as a Navy Seal and Army Ranger compensated for their inexperience with the Bureau.

They both looked muscular and fit, as if they worked out with a lot of weights. I felt like the odd man out, given the testosterone level of these two warriors. I did feel confident, however, that whatever we came across would be expertly handled.

The supervisor assigned our newly formed team of three to South Palm Beach County to search two condominiums in Delray Beach where some of the hijackers reportedly lived. These areas bordered to the south of Boynton Beach where I lived. Knowing these terrorists had lived so close to me personally shocked me even more.

One of our assigned condos, the Hamlet Country Club in West Delray, was where Marwan al-Shehhi lived. He was later identified as another pilot and the one who possibly flew United Airlines Flight 175 into the South Tower of the WTC.

So, near midnight on September 11, I headed out to meet my partners as they brought their FBI car from the rear parking lot to begin our assignments.

After "Seal" and "Ranger" drove up, I loaded my gear into the rear seat. I then climbed in and sat next to my equipment.

None of us spoke during the drive to the Hamlet Country Club. I looked out the window, lost in thought. The information from the briefing had ramped up my emotions. Righteous anger inundated my entire being. I pondered the horrific attack that my country had suffered. I grieved the loss of so many souls.

Once we pulled into the entrance of the country club, the three of us showed our credentials at the guard gate before being allowed entry into this very upscale golf-course community.

We found the building where Marwan al-Shehhi lived. The lighting from the complex illuminated its beige stucco exterior and barrel-tile roof.

Seal took a large duffle bag out of the trunk. He looked over at me and winked. "Just in case…"

I didn't respond, nor did I ask what was in the bag.

We climbed the stairs to the second-floor apartment, each step taken with trepidation as it took us closer to our designation. What if… what if the condo was rigged with explosives or chemicals?

Ranger knocked on the door. I hoped it was empty and that we weren't going to be ambushed.

The lack of response caused me to breathe easier, but only a little. We were not done with our assignment.

We all jointly decided to break into the apartment. Seal laid his bag down on the gray concrete. He then took out a crowbar and ramming tool, and these two warriors went to work to forcefully breach the door.

I said a silent prayer as my heart pounded hard and fast in my chest. We literally didn't know what we were walking into. Was the condo booby-trapped?

They succeeded in their efforts. Not only did we now have access, but we were still alive and in one piece. My heart slowed, though my legs still felt wobbly after all the stress of wondering if we were facing a life-or-death situation.

Inside the apartment, I looked around, taking it all in. Its dirty beige carpet and cheap, flimsy furniture seemed out of place in this high-end complex. The all-white kitchen sat just beyond the living room.

We conducted an initial cursory search of the apartment to ensure we were safe and that it contained no evidence of any further planned attacks. Then we performed a more thorough search.

The unit wasn't large and contained only one bedroom, so we didn't have a lot to go through. Still, not one personal effect could be found. There were some teabags in a kitchen cabinet but not much else.

We closed the door, secured it with crime-scene tape, and left. My partners contacted the FBI to request the Evidence Response Team (ERT), otherwise known as the crime scene unit, to be deployed. They wanted them to conduct an even more detailed search for evidence that we couldn't collect, such as fingerprints, DNA, and any traces of hazardous materials.

By the time we canvassed the entire neighborhood, it was well after midnight. We knocked on door after door, waking up residents to ask them what had transpired with this hijacker while residing at the Hamlet.

Not one of the neighbors complained when rousted from their sleep. They all wanted to cooperate. When they learned the hijackers had lived amongst them, they were horrified.

We spoke to a lady who lived downstairs. She told us that two men with dark skin and dark hair, who might have been Middle Eastern, lived there. She had seen them coming and going from the apartment and described them as unfriendly. They had given her "mean looks" and made her uncomfortable.

Another neighbor described seeing four to five Middle Eastern men sitting in the pool area together. They talked with each other while looking at a document. Other residents reported that a couple of these men swam in the pool late at night between ten and eleven o'clock.

The president of the neighborhood association opened his home office for us. He located copies of the rental information the hijackers had given him.

He said, "I served in the military in World War II. I gotta tell you… knowing the hijackers planned and plotted some of these terrorist attacks while in my complex has shaken me to my core."

I nodded. "Thank you for getting us this information." I started to walk away before stopping and turning around. The man stood there staring in our direction, but I got the feeling he wasn't looking at us. Like most of us, he was in a state of shock.

I said, "And thank you, Sir, for your service."

My words seemed to have slapped him out of his trance. He shook his head as if dispelling a bad thought. He focused his eyes on me and gave a quick nod of acknowledgement.

By two-thirty that morning, we had driven a few miles east to the Delray Beach Racquet Club. We were told that three of the hijackers shared this unit, including Atta, the operational leader of the Al-Qaeda attacks.

The rental agent had called the FBI after recognizing some of the pictures of the hijackers on the news. She told them she had rented a condo to some of the terrorists, including Mohamed Atta.

She came outside when we pulled up to the rental office. Her face was ashen and her voice solemn. "Follow me. Their unit is a short walk." She led us to an upstairs unit. Hopefully, we would find some evidence in this apartment.

She gave me the key. Although we had survived the last condo search, I still felt concerned about the potential of triggering an explosive device or releasing hazardous chemicals upon opening this condo.

I told the rental agent, "Please step back over there."

She nodded and did as she was directed.

I put the key in the keyhole and unlocked it before slowly turning the doorknob. Closing my eyes and taking a deep breath, I pushed open the door. Nothing. No bang, no explosives. I was just met with beautiful silence. Involuntarily, I let out a sigh of relief.

After successfully crossing that hurdle, a chill ran down my spine knowing who inhabited this apartment.

The foyer consisted of a long set of stairs that led up to a third floor. The entry door may not have been booby-trapped, but I had no idea what may be at the top of that stairway.

Since I took the lead to open the door, I figured I should maintain it. With each step I climbed, the anticipation built.

Fortunately, when I opened this door, I was met with the same silence as before. Bland and dirty beige carpet acted as the living room flooring. Over to the side sat a worn-out sofa and a couple of chairs covered by beige and brown fabric.

We searched the unit and found it had been cleaned of most personal effects. The only potential evidence we found was the answering machine, but we couldn't understand the foreign language used. We took the recorder and secured the apartment so the ERT could process it for evidence as well.

I later learned that the message on the machine was thought to be from another hijacker before getting on a plane. In the recording, he praised Allah.

Around three-thirty in the morning, we walked around the complex and woke up some of its residents. They all verified seeing the Middle Eastern men.

The neighbor who lived directly below the men reported a brief interaction with two of them. They had accidentally dropped some clothes from their balcony. The items fell onto the lower roof near her unit.

She said, "They wanted to come into my apartment to get them. I felt afraid of them, so I wouldn't let them in."

I later learned that when the ERT performed their search, they discovered a piece of an airline ticket on the roof. Coincidentally, it happened to be in the same place where the neighbor said the clothes were dropped.

By seven-forty-five, my new teammates and I found ourselves back at the FBI building. We wrote our reports on what had happened upon entering the condos, statements from the neighbors during our canvasses, and information obtained from both the first condo president and the rental agent from the second condo.

Since my supervisor was working out of the FBI building to coordinate any state support with the FBI, I had immediate access to him.

After I gave him a verbal account of what had transpired during our search, he informed me that I had been assigned to work with the FBI for the next few weeks.

I nodded, glad to be working on this assignment. It was critical to our country that these incidents and these terrorist thugs be investigated to the fullest.

I headed home around ten a.m., stopping along the way to check on my mom. Gary called to say he found a rental car. He expected to be home by evening.

I was exhausted, but when I tried to sleep, I couldn't find peace. Thinking about how and why we were attacked kept me restless.

Once Gary returned home, I felt better. Having him there relaxed me so I could sleep again.

Anthrax Attack

The next morning, I drove to the Miami FBI Office. As I drove south on I-95, I called Karen to let her know I was on my way to her office. Calling her wasn't unusual. We were close friends, so we talked frequently.

We had a lot in common; we both were dedicated to our job and passionate about our work, and we both had two dogs. However, she was single, whereas I was married.

When I walked into the conference room, Karen scampered over to me with a big smile on her face. Her raised left eyebrow made me pause.

She grabbed my arm and leaned close to my ear. "Floy, you can thank me later, but I've finagled it so that we've been assigned as partners." She giggled, obviously pleased with herself.

I didn't tell Karen that I secretly hoped to be partnered with Seal and Ranger because I enjoyed their eye-candy appeal. However, I never saw either one of them again. They left a great impression on me, proving themselves to be excellent partners for our first and only assignment together.

Karen and I were assigned to a task-force operation focused on locating all of the crop-duster airplanes in South Florida.

The FBI supervisor said, "We have intelligence showing that Mohamed Atta looked into crop-duster airplanes at a small airport in Belle Glade."

At first, my mind couldn't make the connection. Why would the terrorists be interested in crop dusters in an agricultural area in the western part of Palm Beach County?

The supervisor's eyes darted between Karen's and my faces, neither of us catching onto this unnerving scenario.

He continued, "The hijackers had been looking into the possibility of other terrorists loading a crop duster with lethal chemicals. They then would conduct a mass attack by flying over a public outdoor event."

Oh my.

Karen's jaw had dropped in shock. A chill ran down my spine as I envisioned the devastation and carnage such an attack would create. These guys seemed to be hell-bent on destroying every last soul in this country.

I also learned some other astonishing facts that morning. Some of the 9/11 terrorists received flight training at a Palm Beach County Airport. This airfield was located in Lantana, a small town that borders Boynton Beach to the north. I lived about two miles from it.

I received other information that literally hit close to home. Some of the terrorists worked out at the Planet Gym in Boynton Beach. Not only did I own a membership at that same gym, but I lived about a mile away from it. The mere thought that evil had surrounded and invaded my personal territory disgusted me and made me angry.

While all of this was happening, we experienced a personal tragic loss at home. Gary's father, Mr. Carmichael, died of an apparent heart attack. Gary believed he died from a broken heart. We think seeing the 9/11 attacks, seeing how our foreign enemies could attack our country, was more than he could handle.

His passing was devastating. I admired him and respected his service to his country as an Army soldier. But his service didn't stop upon his retirement from the military. He went on to serve his community as an Orange County Deputy.

We were saddened by our loss and for the loss of a man who was a true patriot to the very end.

The Anthrax-Laden Letters

Karen and I spent weeks verifying the locations of crop-duster airplanes. This mission took us to South Homestead and as far west as the Seminole Tribe Air Hangar near Alligator Alley.

Understandably, this case involved all hands on deck because the attacks didn't stop on 9/11. At the time, we believed more terrorist attacks were forthcoming.

Gary came home late one night in October 2001. He told me about an incident involving Bob Stevens, an employee of American Media's tabloid *The Sun* located in Palm Beach County's Boca Raton. (American Media also published the *National Enquirer*.) Stevens had handled a letter at his workplace that contained anthrax spores and died as a result.

This became a joint case between the FBI and FDLE. Since Gary was assigned to the Palm Beach FDLE office, he was sent to Stevens' house in Lantana, a mere two miles from our home.

Since I had already been working with the FBI, my supervisor assigned me to the Palm Beach FBI task force investigating the anthrax case that killed Mr. Stevens. So, Gary and I ended up working this case together.

Practically overnight, the FBI established a temporary office on the second floor of a building in downtown West Palm Beach. It was vacant and had enough space to serve as a viable working place for a hundred investigators and support staff.

The anthrax-laden letters had infected several more employees of American Media. They had also been mailed to other parts of the country, killing others and sickening even more.

All of us involved in this case were offered Ciprofloxacin, a strong antibiotic utilized by the Florida Department of Health. The drug thwarted off the illness that accompanied exposure to anthrax powder.

Gary and I joined a long line of investigators at a temporary office in West Palm Beach to receive the pills. We kept them in our cars in case we began to feel ill.

The Anthrax Investigation

South Florida remained hypersensitive to the terrorists who had lived in the area. The reported anthrax cases intensified the apprehension, putting everyone on high alert.

Karen and I obtained multiple assignments. These involved interviews, including the newspaper's work associates and possible enemies. Hopefully, someone would say something to lead us to the perpetrator responsible for lacing the letters with anthrax.

Some of those on the list of associates turned out not to have any known grudges against the paper of the victims. In fact, their interactions with the company were positive, so I was able to eliminate those possible suspects. Ruling them out was an important part of the process. Unfortunately, I didn't obtain anything that would help me determine who had perpetrated this crime.

Whoever this madman was, he had successfully murdered many people and deeply affected the lives of those close to his victims.

Through years of investigations, the Department of Justice discovered him to be an Army microbiologist. Years later, while the FBI prepared the charges to indict this person, he committed suicide.

Antiterrorism Task Force

When I returned to work in Fort Lauderdale, Karen called me to tell me she was being moved from Crimes Against Children to the FBI's counterterrorism squad.

Simultaneously, I found myself assigned to an antiterrorism task force. It differed from Karen's task force in that it was a multi-agency investigative team that included about fifteen agents and detectives from the Bureau of Alcohol, Tobacco, Firearms, and Explosives (ATF), the FBI, the Broward Sheriff's Office (BSO), the Palm Beach County Sheriff's Office (PBCSO), and the FDLE. I was glad to be on the front lines with this task force.

My two partners were ATF agents and former FDLE agents whom I knew very well. Not only did both have the same name—Vance—but they possessed great tactical and investigative skills. I really liked them.

Not long after my assignment began, a Middle Eastern woman called the ATF. She said she had valuable information about possible suspects who were engaged in money laundering to support terrorist groups located in various countries. She was a second-generation American from a Middle Eastern family.

This tip was then sent to my task force, and Vance B. was assigned the lead. The woman agreed to cooperate with us as an informant.

In my dealings with informants, I came to realize that many were deceptive with hidden agendas. Often, a potential informant would initiate phone contact but changed his or her mind once they were debriefed and learned what would be expected of them when they brought criminal information to the investigator.

For this reason, the investigator was required to validate the informant's information and the motive for giving it. The most common motivators were revenge and money. Other reasons included trying to become part of the investigation to discover what the agents were learning, to provide inaccurate or misleading information, glamour, and/or excitement. Whatever the cause, the information would always be verified.

The day Vance B. brought this female informant into our office, he asked me to sit in on their interview. She worked at a high-powered South Florida financial firm where she could access sensitive information, such as social security numbers as well as government and possible military information.

I felt like I was observing a modern-day Mata Hari. Her demeanor seemed false, and she made me uneasy. I didn't trust her and couldn't figure out her motive for coming to us. I thought she might be a double agent, telling us what she thought we wanted to hear while attempting to gain information from us. She didn't give us anything of value.

As they wound down the interview, she said, "I feel terrible about the people who lost their lives at the World Trade Center, but the Pentagon was fair game."

We were all pretty good poker players, able to keep a straight face. This, however, took us all off guard. Our jaws dropped in shock as we momentarily froze, trying to make sense out of her cold, cruel words. The interview ended.

I was fuming from her statements. The agents quickly ushered her out of the interview room. Now that she knew our location, our office had become compromised. We knew we could all become victims of counter-surveillance, so we prepared to move.

Hindering the Flow of Terrorist Money

Soon after the 9/11 events, we realized that organized groups of terrorists lived and worked in the United States to make money to further their cause. This led to the development of an investigative strategy for intercepting those funds and disrupting the terrorist organizations.

Our strategy began with a biweekly garbage hunt. Once a target had been established, we notified waste management. They then dropped the contents of their truck, which included that target's trash, in a covered bay at their headquarters. Because garbage has no expectation of privacy, we could freely hunt through the target's discarded belongings without a court order or warrant. Of course, we always wore protective coverings.

This exercise confirmed how people and businesses were creatures of habit, which made our job a little easier. For example, they used the same garbage bags. Whereas one store might utilize heavy black bags, another one used white ones. A peek into one bag would tell us if it was from a dentist or CPA office. We became very adept at spotting our bounty and retrieved a lot of financial records.

We experienced difficulties with one of the food stores we had under surveillance. After a couple of weeks, it seemed that the more we watched them, the more they spotted us and made us as cops.

Then an idea came to me. What if we set up a hotdog stand across the street from the market with two male ATF agents manning the cart?

My colleagues agreed to try my idea. Before long, those hotdog vendors (a.k.a. ATF agents) were collecting about twenty bucks from each of us during the lunch hour. We almost kept them too busy for them to capture the license plate numbers and states from the cars stopping at the store.

We all enjoyed this new business venture and found ourselves to be decent entrepreneurs. Then a county-code enforcer, responsible for making sure street vendors possessed the proper licensure, drove by our hotdog stand. We held our breath. We came close to getting busted, but fortunately, we didn't.

Along with our trash detail and hotdog stand venture, we were given another investigative effort. This assignment involved small grocery stores we called the "Stop and Robs." Several of them were in poorer neighborhoods. We learned that some of the terrorist targets we developed during our investigation owned many of these stores.

We took turns going undercover and using EBT cards to purchase items like beer and cigarettes. We also bought counterfeit movies by the dozen.

The problem with accepting our method of payment was that they engaged in fraudulent activity. The state's Electronic Benefit Transfer (EBT) system gave these payment cards to welfare recipients to buy food or obtain cash. The state prohibited the use of EBT cards to buy items such as beer, cigarettes, and pirated movies.

We suspected some of the stores were involved in money laundering, sending the proceeds to the Middle East to support terrorists. If these stores had a high number of EBT purchases but only a few cans of food on the shelves, we looked deeper into the establishment. We checked to see if a lot of the food that was allegedly bought was actually beer and cigarettes. Confirming this triggered further investigation.

We used whatever innovative techniques we could to achieve our ultimate goal—to disrupt their organization and hinder the flow of money, especially since money laundering was often difficult to track.

One method used was to go undercover and sell them untaxed cigarettes. If they bought them, we subsequently obtained arrest warrants and served them a few days later.

By charging our suspects with the fraudulent crimes of buying untaxed cigarettes, we hoped to discover and track their money trails.

<u>Ground Zero</u>

My first post-9/11 trip to New York took place the second week in December, three months after the attack. Coincidentally, prior to 9/11, Gary had already arranged a surprise vacation to New York City around that same time.

For years prior to 9/11, Gary had been working closely on other assignments with the New York State Police, such as the New York Governor's protective squad when he visited Florida, and some organized crime cases where Florida and New York were connected. Gary was able to have the New York State Police pick us up in Manhattan. They drove us to Ground Zero's viewing stand, a wooden structure that allowed police and first responders to see the recovery and removal site.

I had mixed emotions of going to the site. This was supposed to be our vacation, a time of relaxation and fun. But now was not the time for either, and I was compelled to see this area. Maybe when I did, I could come to terms with what had happened; that I would somehow get closure.

I stared out the window, a lump growing in my throat and a knot twisting in my stomach as we got closer. The emotional mixture continued as part of me felt obliged to see the devastation left behind by ruthless monsters, while the other part wanted to jump out of the car and run the other way.

When we neared the site, I noticed a commotion. Our driver tried to weave in and out of traffic due to massive shutdowns and roads blocked by large trucks full of debris of what was left of the World Trade Center.

Upon our arrival, the utter destruction before our eyes took my breath away and created a solemn atmosphere. The sadness escalated as Gary and I watched a recovery team remove a body from the rubble. We both dropped our heads in prayer, tears falling from our eyes.

We lumbered over to the viewing stand and climbed the stairs to the plywood platform near where the towers once stood tall and proud. Gary and I took out the FDLE uniform patch we had brought. My heart swelled with pride as I saw how other police and firefighters from all over the country had also come and paid their respects. They had placed tokens, like miniature badges, on the plywood platform and tacked their departments' patches to its wall as a sign of unity for those police and firefighters who had lost their lives.

So, we followed suit and used a push pin to tack our patches next to theirs.

<u>Following the Money Laundering Trail</u>

As it turned out, New York City had not seen the last of me. As my task force developed more leads, the year 2002 found me there a few more times.

My ATF partners and I ended up working out of the Manhattan DEA Office. Some of our identified targets from South Florida were linked to past investigative cases with the DEA in New York City via the NCIC (National Crime Information Center). These files were held in the DEA's office. Our task force needed to search them for possible suspects and gain knowledge of their past suspected crimes.

The DEA Office appeared to have outgrown its already small space. In fact, it wasn't big enough for the DEA, let alone the rest of us, try as they might to stuff everything (and everyone) into its tiny confines.

The boxes of case files that were crammed together narrowed the walkway between cubicles. To make matters worse, agents loaded these cubicles with extra clothing and personal items. Maybe the overcrowding caused its dilapidated condition, but a good cleaning on the dirty walls and carpet wouldn't have hurt.

Cathy Mueller from the Florida Office of the Statewide Prosecutor joined our joint task force. Having another female included in one of these trips made me thankful.

Our team made a lot of progress. We developed leads from some suspects who also had federal narcotics charges and suspected criminal activities that the DEA in New York City investigated.

We felt honored to be supporting the efforts to combat the 9/11 attacks from ever happening again. Our actions may have been a small piece of the big picture, and I didn't feel like they compared to what our military battled in a land faraway.

Regardless of the significance of my role, I wanted—needed—to be part of this war against evil.

Remembering the Victims of 9/11

Every trip I made that year to New York City flew by, with each lasting around four days.

My task force had now grown to five—the two Vances, Cathy Mueller, a BSO detective who joined us shortly after the initial trip, and me. Whenever we came to New York, we always made a point to visit Ground Zero to pay tribute to the victims.

The first time I walked this area was with Gary about three months before. I remembered how homemade posters covered the fences, including the ones around Saint Paul's Chapel. Families had placed pictures of missing loved ones in the hopes of finding them or of loved ones who had been killed to honor them.

Now, six months had passed since 9/11. We marveled at how the site had changed. Messages on the fencing had been taken down; the towers' area had been cleared of much of the debris; the initial viewing stand was gone, with a new viewing stand for first responders and families having been erected in another location. There were new memorials in the church where first responders had slept in the pews.

Standing on Ground Zero always caused us to choke up as we remembered the victims of 9/11. This time, however, was different… more emotional. We had finished this part of our assignment, and we knew we wouldn't be back to New York City, back to this place, at least not for work.

We ignored the bitter cold and rain as we stepped outside our SUVs. A shiver ran through my body, and I knew it had nothing to do with the weather.

We knelt in front of the "hole," the spot where the towers had fallen. It looked like a deep impression in the middle of the rubble. Multiple cranes, steel girders, and half-shell buildings could be seen in the background.

I looked around as we stood on the twelve-by-twenty-four-foot plywood platform. I reflected on the twenty-three wreaths hanging on the railing, wrapped in blue ribbon, and sprinkled with white flowers. They represented each of the twenty-three New York City police officers who had died that day.

As a member of law enforcement, I couldn't help but be moved with its symbolism of the thin blue line, one that I would always belong to and love. For me, this was personal because they were my brothers and sisters.

Sadly, over seventy law enforcement died during this tragic event. They represented seven federal, state, and local agencies. Many more heroes have since died as a result of breathing in toxins in the efforts to rescue more victims in 9/11's aftermath.

The cold March wind whipped across my face. I reached up and touched my cheek, feeling a wet film covering it. I couldn't tell if the dampness came from the rain or from tears. Maybe both.

I stared at the remains. For as long as I lived, I would never understand the reason behind the destruction and carnage created by those terrorists on 9/11. But I did understand the ultimate sacrifices made by these heroes to help others and save lives.

The blood of my brothers and sisters in blue cried out for justice. My hands clenched into fists as I crammed them into my coat pockets.

This memorial constructed for law enforcement beckoned me. It didn't just want my tears; it demanded more.

I nodded in understanding as I submitted to its unspoken plea—to never forgot all of the first responders who were murdered on 9/11.

CHAPTER TWO

SERIAL KILLER AILEEN WOURNOS

My flight from New York City became a bumpy ride with frequent eruptions of lightning and thunder. I sat in coach, too eager to get home to see Gary and my dogs to be bothered by turbulence.

So, when the pilot announced our landing would be delayed, I was a bit disappointed. When he informed us the Palm Beach Airport had been closed due to an unknown incident, I then became curious.

Airports didn't just shut down. Something had to be wrong, but what?

While I pondered the possibilities, a flight attendant requested that I follow her to speak with the captain. Maybe this is how I would find out.

I knew her request was official business. After all, I was legally carrying a firearm while flying. TSA always advised the flight crew of any armed passengers and their seat numbers.

To say my curiosity had heightened quite a bit by now was an understatement. I got out of my seat and let the attendant lead the way.

She ushered me through the first-class cabin and into the cockpit. Upon entering, my eyes fell on the massive windshield before me and then on the two men who sat in front of it.

One pilot with graying hair turned his large frame around, his blue eyes analyzing me. The deep wrinkles on his forehead made him look to be in his late fifties. He emitted a confidence that came from being well-seasoned.

The reddish-blonde head that belonged to the copilot remained fixed on the view in front of him. He had taken sole responsibility for flying the plane. I got the feeling the captain had placed his entire focus on me.

The older pilot said, "A passenger in first class refuses to stay in his seat. If the man in seat 4-A gets up again, I want him arrested."

I could barely steady myself with all the bumps, and now he expected me to make an arrest?

I assessed the information given. From what the captain told me, this passenger wasn't obeying verbal instructions. Therefore, he was a serious safety issue and could be arrested for federal offenses.

The captain had the authority to secure any person who presented a threat to the safety of the airplane. However, I was out of my jurisdiction, so I would have to detain the passenger until the feds arrived to relieve me of him.

Then it hit me. *I don't have handcuffs with me. I've only got my Glock and extra magazines.*

I said, "I need some flex cuffs."

The captain ordered the flight attendant to find me some.

While we waited, my prayers were answered, but not in the way I had hoped. The flight attendant returned to notify the captain of a woman in first class who was having difficulty breathing.

"I think she's had a heart attack," she said.

I left the cockpit to check on her. Fortunately, a doctor seated nearby had begun to examine her.

Another flight attendant bent down close to my ear and whispered, "The captain wants you to sit closer to first class." She then crammed a set of flex cuffs in my hand.

I glanced down at my gift and then shoved them in my pocket. I then followed the flight attendant to an empty seat in the second row of the first-class section.

This was not what I had in mind for riding in first class.

I had just got settled in when the flight attendant came over the speaker system to announce that the air traffic controllers cleared our plane to land because of the medical emergency.

Upon landing, fire rescue came aboard and took the ill lady off the plane. We were not allowed to disembark for another hour.

While waiting, I called one of my task force members from the Palm Beach County Sheriff's Office. I asked him what was going on at the airport.

He said, "I'm actually here now. Seems a Secret Service agent didn't inform TSA of the mock incendiary device he had in his carry-on luggage."

This mishap closed the airport for over an hour while he sorted it out with TSA.

Hopefully, this Secret Service agent learned his lesson; I know I did. From that point on, if I flew armed, I carried my lightweight metal handcuffs in my bag.

The Nautical Life

During my time assigned to the antiterrorism squad, I realized that the American dream had been shattered by the attack on our homeland. This realization, coupled with our love of being on the water, led Gary and me to make a life-changing decision. We started the process of living on a boat and becoming fulltime "liveaboards."

We owned a twenty-foot-console runabout that we played on just about every weekend we were together. We enjoyed it so much. Life was too short to not enjoy the best things Florida living had to offer. In addition, we wanted to be free to live with fewer burdens.

Now that it was just the three of us—Gary, Little Bit, and me—we thought it was the perfect time for us to go forth with our plans. Sadly, our one-hundred-twenty-pound Rottweiler, Hardy, had developed cancer and was in pain, so we had to put him down. I now understood why God had sent us Little Bit. She became such a comfort while we mourned over Hardy.

So, without a need for a backyard for two dogs, we realized we could manage a dog of Little Bit's size on the boat. Within a two-month period, we sold our house. We then took two weeks off from work, put our furniture in a rental truck, and drove to Atlanta to give some of it to my youngest daughter and then across the country to give the remainder to my oldest daughter.

With that out of the way, we sold our runabout and purchased a forty-three-foot Ocean Alexander trawler in Vero Beach and moved aboard. Its twin six-cylinder diesel engines powered it to the Palm Harbor Marina located on the Intercoastal Waterway in downtown West Palm Beach.

We officially christened our new home the *C-Breeze*. Not only was it functional, but aesthetically, it was beautiful.

The boat was designed by the famous American Marine Architect Ed Monk and built in Taiwan in 1985. It came with a good-sized saloon, lower galley, beam-to-beam master stateroom, a large forward V-berth, and two complete heads (bathrooms) with shower stalls tall enough for Gary to comfortably stand. Brass accents complemented the teak interior walls, teak flooring, and teak cabinetry. A large aft sun-deck and upper and lower helm stations finished off the structure.

The teak exterior decking gave Little Bit excellent footing while we were underway. She took to boating life very well except that she never learned to do her personal business onboard.

During the first year we lived on the boat, we talked to many other boaters with onboard pets. We sought advice about training her, but nothing worked as well for her as getting off the boat. She felt the most comfortable when back on good ole dirt or grass to take care of her personal needs.

Little Bit became our first line of security. Nobody could approach the boat while at the dock or anchored offshore without her alerting us. She developed her special vantage points either up on the flybridge or on the aft (rear) deck. She positioned herself in strategic locations where she could see everything, giving us a great sense of reassurance. Everyone in the marinas where we lived over the years got to know Little Bit.

On a few occasions at certain marinas, we knew to be especially watchful. At times, when the tides rose just right, our main deck would be positioned at the same level as the dock. Little Bit took this opportunity to jump off the boat and visit the neighbors.

Always on the lookout for treats, she seemed to know exactly which boats would welcome her aboard. She never went far and always returned with her tail wagging. She expected us to be just as happy as she was about her adventures.

Many times, our neighbors hailed us via radio to alert us that she had gotten off our boat to visit them. Little Bit especially enjoyed visiting those neighbors with cats aboard. She loved feisty kitties. She never went aboard those "cat boats," but she loved to sit dockside and stare them down. Most cats gave her little attention, though.

Our heavy-duty well-built trawler vessel, along with Little Bit performing her outstanding security duties, gave us a feeling of security.

We wanted a change of lifestyle, and we got it. In hindsight, I'm not certain we experienced fewer burdens living aboard a boat rather than on land. Regardless, we enjoyed this adventure for many years.

Escorting a Serial Killer

After arriving from my last New York task force trip and walking through the Miami airport, my cell phone started ringing. I pulled it out of my pocket and clicked the answer button.

"Floy, this is Warden Carol Rodriquez from Broward Correctional Institution. I know you've spoken to Aileen Wuornos on some of your visits to the prison. Would you consider being part of the team to move her to death row at Florida State Prison?"

I stopped walking as I processed her request. She paused for a moment as if to give me that moment.

I flashed back to those times when I talked to Aileen. Admittedly, I felt conflicted about the request to transport her to her execution. On one hand, she was a serial murderer, and families had lost loved ones; on the other, she had endured a terrible life. I shook my head, thinking about how sad of a situation this was.

Warden Rodriquez continued while other travelers passed by me. "I want an FDLE agent to accompany Aileen since she's made several allegations that the prison guards have mistreated her. I've already spoken to the FDLE command in Tallahassee. They agreed and referred me to the Miami SAC. I spoke to him earlier, and he's cleared your involvement with the move."

That same conflict persisted. Still, I felt it was my job. "Okay, I'll do it."

This would be a difficult assignment emotionally, but my duty as a public servant didn't allow room for emotions; it required me to follow through to the best of my ability.

Warden Rodriquez asked, "Good. Can you meet me at my prison at two o'clock in the morning?"

I grimaced at the early hour. It was protocol to move inmates, especially high-profile ones, in the middle of the night. It was quicker and tactically safer if done as soon as approved. There was less chance people would find out about it.

Glancing at my watch, I quickly calculated in my mind that in just a few hours, I needed to report to the prison. That gave me a short window to eat dinner and catch some sleep.

I took a deep breathe. "Sure. See you then."

That night, I set my alarm clock for a midnight wake-up call. I felt like I had just fallen asleep when the buzzer went off. I pulled myself out of bed and took a quick shower before dressing in casual-business clothes with a jacket and boots. Since I'd be riding in a prison van from Fort Lauderdale to Starke and back for close to eight hundred miles round trip, I wanted to be comfortable.

As I stepped outside into the dark night, the humidity attacked me immediately, dragging mugginess with it. There were no stars overhead, and I realized dark clouds must be covering the sky. The marina lights provided the only illumination for my walk alone down the boat dock.

The old wooden planks made a soft creaking noise with each step I took. The lapping sound of water against the pilings further created the eerie feeling that plagued me. In my mind, I prepared myself for waking up Aileen and telling her where she was headed.

During my hour-long drive to the prison, I thought about the fate that awaited Aileen in Starke. Too soon, I saw exterior lights in the distance illuminating the prison buildings and grounds. It looked like a bright island in the middle of a dark area just east of the Everglades. However, what resided behind those gray concrete walls emanated anything but light.

I felt apprehensive about facing Aileen with what would be her last ride. I knew she had requested her execution not be delayed any further.

I approached the prison entry checkpoint. Warden Rodriquez stood almost as tall as the guard she stood next to. Her short brown hair outlined her round face, and the end of her bangs touched the top of her wire-framed glasses.

She wore a navy-blue skirt and pale-yellow blouse with a red sweater draped over her wide shoulders. Her black lace-up shoes gave her a mature and matronly appeal.

She showed no emotion as she explained the procedure. "After we wake up Aileen, we'll need to give her a few minutes to get dressed. Then we'll remove her from the solitary confinement section to the garage where two vans are lined up for the trip and waiting. I've assigned four prison guards for the transfer detail, two in each van."

I nodded in understanding.

Still saddened by the circumstances, I followed Warden Rodriguez along a narrow walkway lined with a high fence crowned by razor wire. When we arrived at the entrance to the main jail, a prison guard was sitting behind a bulletproof window. Close by were heavy, gray iron doors that not only kept the unvetted out but acted as another obstacle to keep the prisoners in.

I showed my credentials to the guard and signed into the prison.

A loud buzzer sounded, and the heavy automatic steel door opened with a loud thud. We walked into the main prison. The door closed behind us with another thud. After being in so many jails and prisons, I had become desensitized to that sound.

We crossed an area near the small prison store where inmates purchase approved items. We kept walking. Our shoes sounded loud as they hit the bare concrete floor. I shivered from the damp cold environment inside the cell block.

We came to another secure door. Because of the high security level required in prisons, another guard inspected my credentials before clearing us to enter through that second door. We then stepped into the area that housed inmates in solitary confinement.

Here, about half a dozen solid, heavy metal doors contained a slit about face level. Guards spoke to the inmates through those small apertures.

A guard opened Aileen's cell door. A dim light streaming in from the hallway allowed me to see her outline on a very low bed. She seemed to be sleeping on her side facing us. The guard flipped the light switch, illuminating her cell.

My eyes reacted to the sudden appearance of the bright lights. I squinted as Aileen slowly became aware that her cell had filled up with light and people. She rose up on one arm and held her other forearm over her eyes to shield them from the glare.

Warden Rodriquez said, "Aileen, you need to get ready for the trip to Florida State Prison."

To my utter perplexity, Aileen began to giggle and laugh. She gathered her belongings, which wasn't a lot. From previous interactions with inmates, I knew they treasured their small assortment of allowed personal items. Those on the outside may not consider those types of things important, but to a prisoner, they can be all they own in the world. Of course, we had to double check what she took to make sure there wasn't any contraband.

Everyone left the cell to give Aileen a few minutes of privacy. We left her door open while she got dressed in her orange prison jumpsuit and groomed herself for travel.

A few minutes later, we heard her say, "I'm ready."

Aileen walked next to me with her head up. Despite the reason for our trip, she seemed fine with leaving.

We made our way to a confined garage area where two vans waited. Aileen and I climbed into the back seat of the second van; the first van would take on the role of security.

Moving an inmate to death row is a dangerous assignment and never taken lightly. I felt secure because this case was high-profile, and the warden would only select the most trusted and experienced officers for this detail.

I had given my firearm to a guard when I entered the prison. He then passed it onto one of the transport guards, who put it in a lockbox in the front of the van. Because I would be in close proximity to a prisoner, I couldn't have my gun on my person.

Aileen and I didn't discuss her case or anything about her execution. Instead, I made simple conversation as if we were two strangers on a bus ride to Detroit, even though that couldn't be further from the truth.

I turned my head to look at her. "Do you remember me? I'm an FDLE agent."

Her eyes briefly opened wide with recognition. A big smile spread across her face. "Yes, I do. How is Sniffer doing?"

I returned her smile. "Fine."

Sniffer was the K-9 handled by my partner Jacob when I was a trooper with the Florida Highway Patrol a lifetime ago. When we occasionally came to the prison to conduct searches, we always made an effort to visit Aileen because she always lit up when she saw Sniffer.

Her upbeat attitude concerned me. She was going to her death, yet she treated it as no big deal. In fact, she kept a big smile on her face and her eyes remained wide. She laughed and became giddy for no reason.

I wondered if she really understood her situation. I can only imagine how I would feel if I were headed to my execution. I wouldn't be laughing, that's for sure. Then I thought she could be displaying a nervous reaction.

A part of me still felt sorry for Aileen, even though I was on the side of justice. She was convicted of killing six men, all of whom were believed to have been her johns. These despicable crimes caused untold grief for the families of the people she murdered.

I must concede that I'll always believe Aileen was the victim of a cruel and miserable life. She wasn't nurtured or loved during her formative years. After she was born, her father was incarcerated for life after being convicted of sex crimes against children. While in prison, he hung himself. Then Aileen's mother abandoned her when she was very young.

She began to sell herself for sex at the age of nine, a time when most little girls are still playing with dolls. She exchanged sexual encounters for cigarettes, food, and drugs. At thirteen, her grandfather's friend raped and impregnated her. Her grandparents sent her away to have the baby. Then they gave her baby girl up for adoption.

Everyone in the van rode in silence. Looking out into the stillness of the night, I observed the changes in the terrain as we traveled north on the Florida Turnpike. The flatness of the land gave way to slight hills. By the time we reached Interstate 75 (I-75) northwest of Orlando, the moonlight allowed me to see the silhouettes of the moss-bearing oak trees.

When we neared Ocala, we stopped at the Lowell Correctional Institution, a large prison, for food and a bathroom break. I learned later on that the primary women's state prison in Broward would be moved to this complex.

The sun was coming up. A few rays of sunshine peeked across the tree lines as we proceeded up the prison's winding driveway.

I told Aileen we were stopping for a bathroom break and breakfast. She nodded and smiled.

When we pulled up in front of the main entrance, the prison inspector greeted us. He then ushered us into a small private area just outside the major prison complex.

Aileen trudged in front of me, her handcuffs and leg chains threaded through a waist chain.

We walked through the designated doorway and onto gray linoleum flooring. I looked around the room, my eyes quickly making mental notes of its layout.

Its size looked adequate to hold visitors waiting to see loved ones or for employee-training purposes. Formica-covered tables and blue plastic chairs provided the only furnishings.

After locating the ladies' restroom, I turned to Aileen, removed her handcuffs and handed them to a guard. However, the chains remained on her legs.

As soon as we entered the ladies' room, I searched all four of its stalls and settled on one. I held the stall door open. "Go ahead and use this one, but leave it unlocked." I then waited near the sinks.

We went back to the room and found two seats. I opened one of the brown bags lying on the table and pulled out its contents: a fried egg sandwich, a banana, two cookies, coffee, and a soft drink.

I drank the weak coffee after adding powdered creamer that refused to completely dissolve. I declined my egg dish and located a power bar in the pocket of my jacket. I choked down the bar while gulping the remainder of my coffee.

Fortunately, I wasn't sleepy or tired. As an FDLE special agent, I was used to working odd hours. My body was used to getting little sleep.

We then piled back into the vans and headed further north, traveling on U.S. 301 into Starke. Finally, our almost-four-hundred-mile trip with Aileen had come to an end.

Upon entering the prison vicinity, we passed underneath a metal arch with the words *Florida State Prison* welded onto it. We stopped at the manned guard gate and presented our credentials and necessary paperwork before driving into the fenced-in area topped with razor wire.

Our convoy pulled up to the main building of this massive tan-colored complex. A burly man with slicked-back black hair and glasses stood in front of the main building. He looked official in his short-sleeve white shirt, blue tie, and casual dress slacks.

We all exited the vans. I couldn't help but give an involuntary stretch. Aileen acted fine.

The official-looking man walked over to us and introduced himself as the warden. He gave us a genuine smile as he welcomed all of us. He then greeted Aileen by her first name.

We all followed behind the warden through a maze of beige-colored walls and bare concrete floors. We walked by three death-row cell blocks where its male inmates lived. Thick sheets of plexiglass and iron bars enclosed those who have committed horrible crimes.

Finally, we entered a small isolated area. Since Aileen was the only woman, she would be housed by herself as she awaited execution.

She walked into the small, drab, bare cell enclosed by beige bars. It had just enough space to hold a small bed, a sink, and a toilet. It was a sad place, and the dingy-gray color choice reflected this.

The warden's gaze on Aileen didn't falter as he tilted his head toward a uniformed, heavyset, middle-aged woman. "This officer's been assigned to monitor you. If there's anything you need, just let her know." He spoke with kindness.

I watched the scene in front of me. Realizing this was the last place Aileen would live on earth, I remained amazed by her calm demeanor. I figured the warden assigned a female correction officer because of Aileen's reputation of accusing male guards of harassing her, and he didn't want any complaints. Plus, he probably thought she would feel more comfortable with a woman.

The warden broke into my thoughts. "Agent Turner, will you please come with me?"

I turned my eyes to the warden and nodded. I followed him to his office. I didn't speak to Aileen; I didn't know what to say.

The warden thanked me for my time and efforts with the transfer. "You're welcome to come back and view the execution," he said.

Since I had known Aileen, I really didn't want to see the execution. I felt the event would be too morbid, and I had no valid reason to attend.

I gave a half-smile and shook my head. "Thanks, but I think I'll pass."

I left the warden's office and returned to the van. The experience left me feeling empty, worn out, and sad. I crawled into the backseat and stared out the window. The Broward County guards were waiting for me. They handed me back my gun.

I stared out the window as we drove away, although I don't remember what I was looking at. I kept seeing Aileen's smile and giddiness.

The officer driving my van broke into my thoughts. "Who wants to eat a big breakfast in Gainesville?"

I jumped at the thought of a good cup of coffee, as I hadn't eaten anything but a power bar the night before. "Sounds good to me."

The other guard said, "Man, I could use some food. I'll check with the other van."

He radioed our intentions to the guards in the other van and immediately acquired positive responses. We were off to a mom-and-pop place known by the correctional officers.

I felt relieved to be putting a few miles between myself and the prison. As we neared the diner, I felt my hunger grow, but the lump in my throat mitigated that primal urge.

Since I had gotten to know Aileen, the conflict between compassion for her inevitable death and justice for the victims, their families, and friends constantly tugged at my emotions. I realized how brutal the burden of justice was on those of us who were required to carry it, and I didn't take the death sentence lightly.

When I got back to Fort Lauderdale, I thought about my invite to the execution. FDLE agents assigned to the Executive Investigations Unit in Tallahassee normally witnessed all executions.

Death by lethal injection was now the rule of law for Florida's death row, as Florida retired the electric chair known as "Old Sparky" in 2000. My many years in law enforcement led me to believe that Aileen's execution by lethal injection would be painless.

I knew I had made the right decision to turn down the warden's invitation. I had had enough.

I hoped Aileen was finally at peace. She certainly didn't find it here on Earth.

CHAPTER THREE

A CHRISTMAS KIDNAPPING

The cool December day caused my thoughts to focus on my holiday menu. With Christmas less than a week away, I had to pay more attention to the gifts I needed to buy and the food we would eat for dinner.

Personally, I've always loved this time of year. The music, the ambiance, and how residents adorned their tropical South Florida homes with tinsel, cheap snowmen and reindeer, and various light displays. All that was missing was snow, but that didn't stop some. They used fake snow, which never melted regardless of the temperature.

I didn't even mind the traffic that seemed heavier this time of year. Some of it came from the shoppers and parties, and some of it came from "snowbirds" clogging the local roads. This was a name Floridians gave to tourists who fled the north's cold weather for Florida's warm winters, and we welcomed them with open arms.

Outside of work, I took advantage by getting together with friends and colleagues. I had gotten a Christmas present for my friend, FBI Special Agent Karen Kool.

I called her and suggested we meet for dinner. This would be a great opportunity to give her the gift.

We decided to meet at five-thirty at Houston's Restaurant on Atlantic Boulevard in Pompano Beach. Its proximity to my office and Karen's house always made it a good meeting point.

I arrived first and found us a table before it got busy. I had no sooner started looking at the menu when Karen came bustling in with a big smile and that same twinkle in her eyes.

"Hi, Floy. I hope you haven't been waiting too long," she said. "Traffic going in and out of the mall was gruesome." She then plopped down in her seat. "Oh, yeah," she continued. "I got you this."

She handed me a present encased in white and gold gift wrapping. After ripping off the paper, I pulled a blue ceramic coffee mug with the FBI name and logo etched in gold.

"Thanks, Karen. I love it!" I handed her a small red and green gift bag. "And this is for you."

She raised an eyebrow and gave me a half-smile. "Thanks, Floy."

She reached into her small bag and pulled out a brass-plated key chain with the FDLE logo etched in blue and gold. We laughed as we realized we had given each other typical cop presents.

After exchanging gifts, Karen's cell phone rang. Her smile quickly vanished, and she stared straight at me.

She said to her caller, "No need to call FDLE. Floy's here with me. We were about to order dinner."

I sensed we needed to put dinner on hold.

"I'll check with Floy to see if she can meet with you," she continued.

Karen was still assigned to the counterterrorism squad, which became the forerunner to the Joint Terrorism Task Force (JTTF). It involved a partnership between various federal, state, and local law enforcement agencies required to take action against terrorism. The investigative techniques incorporated by the JTTF included physical and electronic surveillance, confidential source development and interviewing, and other direct proactive police techniques.

After Karen hung up, she said, "Buddy Hank is waiting for us at a marina in Adventura."

I began to quickly gather my belongings. I knew FBI Special Agent Buddy Hank from when we had worked the plastic cocaine investigation together. Between his easy-going demeanor and head-turning good looks, I enjoyed working with him. Now he wanted us to meet him in the extreme northeast section of Miami-Dade County for a case.

Karen placed her phone in her purse. "Buddy needs help investigating an active kidnapping case. A mother and two children have been abducted."

Since my last trip to New York, my investigative efforts had been refocused on my assignment as the FDLE South Regional Crimes Against Children Coordinator. Of course, I was glad to help, and this case appeared to entail some of the qualifying components.

"According to Buddy," Karen said as she picked up her gift bag, "the kidnappers are using a cell phone to demand a ransom from the father. The FBI's using its new electronic tracking techniques that can help identify possible locations where the calls came from. So, we're meeting Buddy at the marina. It's close to where the kidnapper's cell phone has been tracked and across the waterway from the victims' condo in Sunny Isles."

Our tanned and buffed-looking young male waiter must have seen us leaving. He rushed over to us. "Ladies, you aren't leaving us, are you?"

Karen and I glanced at each other with a smile of disappointment. She said, "We are so, so sorry and would love to stay, but yes, we have to leave. Appears our dinners plans have changed."

We then bolted out to our cars.

During the twenty-minute drive south to Adventura, I called my supervisor. I notified him that the FBI asked me to help them with this developing case.

Following behind Karen, I pulled into the parking lot of a marina in Adventura. I got out of my car and looked up at the clear skies dotted with twinkling stars. I then looked to the east and saw the top of the high-rise on the Intercoastal Waterway where Uri Bassano once lived. That brought back memories of when I worked with the Florida Highway Patrol.

Uri was the subject of a joint DEA-FDLE-FHP case I was involved with as a trooper. I remembered serving a search warrant on his penthouse. I suppressed a laugh as I recalled my fear and concern about Uri seeking revenge for our nosing around in his business and how the justice system kept the million dollars confiscated from him during a car stop. That seemed like a lifetime ago.

Karen and I flashed our credentials to a slim, middle-aged security guard manning the marina security gate. We told him our destination.

"Yes, ma'ams." He pointed to the three-story building in front of the docks that held a variety of boats. "Take the elevator on up to the third floor. You can't miss the lounge."

We thanked him and parked our cars. After entering the vestibule, we saw the elevators straight ahead. When the doors opened to the third floor, I stepped onto a marble floor. My shoes tapped against its hard surface.

Floor-to-ceiling windows greeted me, showing off a gorgeous view of the water. The contrast between the water and sky darkened by the night, the cream-colored window treatments, and the dark-wood antique furniture provided a rich and interesting contrast.

Buddy stood in the middle of my view, his slender build leaning over a high-top table as he wrote in his notebook on the counter's black granite top. Fortunately, he was the only one in the lounge, which ensured our privacy.

"Hi Karen." His expressive, brown eyes landed on me. "And hey there, Floy. Good to see you again. Thanks for agreeing to help."

I smiled. "Good seeing you again, Buddy."

Karen looked at the pad that Buddy was writing on before slowly lifting her eyes to look at him. "So, what's going on?"

"Okay, here's the scoop." He proceeded to fill us in on the facts surrounding the kidnapping. "The family moved from Brazil to Sunny Isles. The dad's very wealthy, owning a computer software business that he's keeping in Brazil.

"At the time of the kidnapping, the eleven-month-old baby boy and nine-year-old son were with their mother. The couple also has a twelve-year-old daughter, but she was with her father when this happened.

Buddy glanced down at his notes. "Last night, the parents went Christmas shopping at the Boca Raton Mall. The father drove his Porsche when they left the family residence.

"Some Brazilian friends, who live in the high-rise building across the street, had invited them to a holiday dinner celebration. The parents had arranged for their nanny to drop them off at the party.

"After dinner, the older son wanted to go home and work on a school project. The mother decided to take both boys home. She planned to walk, but her husband told her to drive the Porsche. He suggested she valet park in front of their building. Instead, the mother drove the Porsche into the garage located under the building. She pulled the car into one of their assigned parking spots.

"When the father arrived home with his daughter, he couldn't find the mother and his sons. His Porsche was in its designated parking slot. His wife's gold luxury SUV was missing. He looked around the area and noticed blood stains on the pavement.

"The father became frantic with worry. After looking around the building, he called the Sunny Isles Police Department.

"Two officers responded. They called in detectives, who conducted interviews and a neighborhood canvass. Crime scene technicians examined the blood and identified it as human."

Buddy looked up at us over the top of his glasses, shifting his weight from one leg to the other.

He continued to read from his report. "Early this morning, the father received a phone call demanding a ransom. A few hours later, he learned a note had been delivered to his office. The note, written in Portuguese, demanded a million-dollar ransom for his family.

"The local police took the father's statement and preserved the note for evidence. Since kidnapping is a federal offense, SIPD detectives called the FBI to inform them of the kidnapping and ransom demands. And that's where we came in."

As I listened intently, I thought about how we needed to take a hard look at the father, interview him, and have him take a polygraph to rule him out. We also needed to develop other leads for other suspects.

Buddy continued, "Karen, would you set up the team who's going to be monitoring and capturing the incoming telephone calls into the penthouse? Also, I need you to serve as the family liaison for the FBI."

She nodded. "I'll get started now. Is there anything else I need to know first?"

"Yeah. The electronic investigation triangulated the incoming calls coming from the kidnappers. They're showing that they're local, calling near the Adventura area."

While Karen was busy writing in her own notepad, Buddy's gaze fell on me. "Floy, would you mind helping us look for the wife's gold SUV?"

"Sure," I said. "Let me go get some things from my car."

Time was of the essence, so I rushed outside, checking in with my supervisor along the way. I conveyed the information that Buddy had given us. My supervisor told me to keep him apprised.

I retrieved my laptop from my car and walked back to the lounge. I opened a case in the FDLE electronic file system and begin the reporting process.

Around ten o'clock, Buddy walked over to me with a tall, slim man. "Floy, this is Detective Paul Schmidt from the SIPD," he said. "He'll be working with us on this case. Since he's familiar with this area, he's going with us to look for the wife's SUV."

I smiled at Detective Schmidt. I guessed him to be in his early forties, and I appreciated his kind eyes as he returned my smile.

The three of us drove around in Buddy's car for several hours. We also requested that the local police keep an eye out for the SUV. We came up empty handed.

Buddy said, "Listen, we're getting nowhere, and it's late. Let's call it a night, go home, and get some much-needed sleep. You guys mind meeting me in the morning at six? We can meet at the SIPD station near the penthouse."

We both agreed to the time and place.

I went home sometime in the wee hours, my body exhausted, but my mind running faster than I drove. When five a.m. came, I opened my eyes and tried to gather my thoughts. I remembered that I was waking up extra early for the kidnapping case.

Stepping outside, the December morning offered a brisk chill. I wrapped my jacket a little tighter around me and rushed to my car to start heating it up.

On my drive to the SIPD station, Karen called. "Hey, Floy, I want you to know that all of the FBI investigative efforts have intensified. We've established and manned a central command center at our headquarters building."

I thanked her and hung up. I had hoped that activities might have lessened during the few hours I slept, which would have meant the case had been solved, and the family had arrived home safe. Obviously, that didn't happen.

When I arrived at the SIPD, I found Buddy sitting alone at a table in one of the interview rooms. He was deep in thought, reading what looked like a report.

He glanced up and gave a half smile. "Mornin', Floy. Have a seat." He pointed to the chair across from him. "Paul called. He got caught up in something and said he'd meet us later. Since we've been gone, appears the father has received a few more calls. In one of the calls, the kidnappers put the mother on the telephone. She cried, telling her husband that if he didn't pay, they would kill her and the boys."

I studied Buddy as I processed this information. His jaw had tensed up, and he rubbed the back of his neck.

Buddy and I headed out to the same area where we searched the previous night. The mobile tech agents had been driving around to get a signal on their new cell-phone tracking-device equipment, so we set a meeting place on the side of the road to brief them on what had developed from the investigation. They could then triangulate the signal based on the recent kidnapper's demands. Although we were certain the calls originated from the cell towers in Adventura, we still hadn't been able to pinpoint the exact location.

Buddy and I were becoming frustrated. We needed more information to locate these victims. We knew from experience that every minute counted in these types of cases.

Karen called us from the family penthouse. She told us that some of the FBI agents took the father to his office on Brickell Avenue. The father was trying to liquidate some assets in case he needed to provide the ransom.

Shortly after noontime, a break came. The technical agents had zeroed in on an Adventura address within the cell-triangulation area.

Buddy contacted Paul to tell him where we were going and why.

Paul said, "I'm on my way. I'll meet you there."

Buddy drove to the location, which turned out to be a large trailer park of about a couple hundred trailers, many of them old and dilapidated. Its roadways consisted of either cracked asphalt or loose gravel. The walkways in disrepair and the lack of greenery gave the impression of a drab, neglected neighborhood. It was local knowledge that most of the residents in this area consisted of French Canadians who flocked to South Florida to avoid the frigid Canadian winters.

We spotted the trailer park's business office right off the main road. Buddy pulled in front and waited for Paul. Within a few minutes, Paul drove up in his unmarked car.

Inside the small, one-room office, a chubby, balding man greeted us and introduced himself as the manager. His oversized black-rimmed glasses clashed with his light complexion. Below a bulbous red-veined nose sat an unlit cigar hanging out of his mouth. A pair of suspenders held up his drooping pants that complemented his well-worn attire.

After Buddy introduced us, he asked, "Have you noticed a gold SUV or any unusual activity in the area?"

The manager's eyes darted between us before answering. "No."

On a hunch, I asked, "Do you have any South American or Hispanic residents in the park?"

He shrugged. "Yeah, a few."

I asked, "Can we look over your rental agreements to see if any of the residents are new?"

He agreed and waddled through an open door to a room that held several file cabinets, shelves, and boxes of different sizes. I watched him grab one of the file boxes to bring into the room.

"Here," he said. "You should be able to find what you need somewhere in this."

We gathered around that file box like three hungry dogs who had just been given a bone. I took out about a third of the files, as did

Buddy and Paul. We then started the task of reviewing his records and hunting for renters with Hispanic names.

By the time we left, we had garnered information on about a half-dozen residents who deserved a closer assessment. We decided to drive around and evaluate their trailers for the slightest hint of unusual activity. Paul climbed into his unmarked police car and headed one way while Buddy drove off in the opposite direction.

We reported our findings to the mobile technical agents. We verified that we were developing suspects in the park that they had zoned in on and that we were taking a closer look.

Those agents then moved their location closer to us and drove around until they could get a clearer track on any more cell calls.

Buddy and I drove to the very rear of the park and behind the trailers. The aesthetics didn't improve any. I noticed an abandoned concrete-block ranch-style house. All of the hurricane shutters were closed, which seemed unusual.

I pointed it out to Buddy. "This place looks abandoned with the hurricane shutters covering the windows, but we're not in hurricane season. So why would the owners leave their house like that? In fact, this entire structure is strange, sitting in a trailer park. I think we need to find out more about it."

Buddy agreed, so I called Paul and told him about our findings. "We're heading back to the park's office. We want to see if this house is part of the park and who, if anyone, is living in it. Meet you there."

We pulled in front of the office at the same time as Paul. Upon entering, I saw the manager back in his chair and talking on the phone.

"Yeah, gotta go now. Somebody just came in," he said to whoever he was talking to on the phone before dropping the receiver into its cradle.

He started to rise from his chair, but Buddy waved him down. Buddy asked, "Hey, that house in the back of the park. What do you know about it?"

"Oh, that place. I rented it to some Hispanic men a few weeks ago. They wanted to use it for storage. No one lives there. It's just an old house."

My antennae popped up, alerting me to the possibilities and placing my mind in overdrive. We had just uncovered a great lead.

With that bit of information, everything came together.

The Rescue

The kidnappers made another telephone call. The tech guys reported back that they were sure the call had originated from inside this old house.

After leaving the trailer park, Buddy called the command team on the way and filled them in on our findings. "Three Hispanic males rented this house at the back of this trailer park, allegedly for storage. The techs believe the last call came from the house. We think this is enough to get a search warrant and have the hostage rescue team gain a forced entry."

We drove to another access road so we could take a look at the house from another angle. Paul went back to his police station, which was nearby. He needed to brief his command staff and m arrange for their officers in marked patrol cars to stay clear of the immediate area.

Armed with this information, the SIPD supervisors and the FBI requested Adventura Police supervisors to secure the entire trailer park and everything within the block surrounding it. They assigned some of their undercover police officers to surveil the perimeter.

Paul rejoined Buddy and me about forty-five minutes later in the back of the trailer park. He found us hiding in some bushes behind the house. From that spot, we had a view of the garage and walkway that led to the side of the house since the front door was covered by a hurricane shutter.

Buddy said, "We're going to send a helicopter to take some pictures for the HRT."

The FBI's HRT (Hostage Rescue Team) was a specialized unit known to offer a tactical resolution option in hostage and high-risk law enforcement situations. It functioned as a national SWAT.

Around one-thirty that afternoon, we wanted to maintain a closer surveillance and get as close as possible. The three of us crab-walked (a low-to-the-ground crawl) behind the house. We then hid behind a small fenced-in area allocated for garbage cans.

We provided a detailed description of the building from our vantage point. We then initiated a vigorous surveillance on this structure and monitored it for any movement, but none happened.

In an ongoing event such as a suspected kidnapping, a search warrant was not legally necessary in order to rescue victims due to exigent circumstances. However, a search warrant would be needed to further search a structure for related evidence once the victims were removed.

A case that used a search warrant to obtain evidence would not likely be challenged in a later trial. Otherwise, a good defense team could come in and challenge discovered evidence with a motion to suppress.

Buddy, Paul, and I ended up maintaining surveillance for ten more hours. During that time, FBI headquarters communicated latest events with Buddy via radio and organized the entry. I couldn't help but think that this was taking a long time and hoping it could move faster.

Two more agents on the HRT team gathered the county and city building records. They reviewed them in-depth to learn the interior layout structure of the home. They could then help plan a safe rescue.

We learned over our radio earpieces that more calls had come into the father. The FBI told Buddy that they had instructed the father to request "proof of life." In doing so, he had to demand to speak with his wife again to make sure she was still alive.

We were unable to confirm whether the victims were inside, but the cell phone triangulation indicated that the calls were coming from there. As a result, about eleven that night, we received notification that other members of the HRT were forming a couple of blocks away. Execution of the house entry would proceed within a few minutes. They would then either apprehend the caller and rescue the mom and kids or rule out the house.

I asked Buddy, "Since there might be a small baby inside, will the entry team use flashbang grenades when they go into the house?"

A flashbang grenade was a throwable device that once deployed, created a loud noise and a concussion explosion. SWAT teams used this to cause distraction because the perp's focus would be transferred onto the flashbang.

Buddy shrugged. "Nahh. I don't think they'll use a flashbang."

Before I knew it, a dozen officers arrived dressed in SWAT uniforms. They breached the back door. One of them used a special type of gun to shoot a flashbang grenade into the house.

Buddy got that one wrong. My ears rang so badly, I could hardly hear. I could only imagine the victims' shock if they were inside as these concussion grenades exploded.

As soon as the team entered the house, I heard the shrill screams of a woman as if she was being tortured or absolutely terrified. At this point, I didn't know which one. My heart raced with anticipation as Buddy, Paul, and I ran over to the front lawn.

One by one, HRT members exited the house from the side door. The first one carried this frightened and still screaming woman. Behind her, I saw another HRT member carrying the young boy. Seeing his wide-eyed expression revealing fear and confusion, I was sorry they had to endure this horrific event. I worried about the trauma that would undoubtedly stay with them for years to come.

Then I saw the baby. He was bundled and carried in the arms of a strong FBI warrior wearing a bulletproof helmet, safety glasses draped over his chest, a Balaclava (mask) covering most of his face, black gloves on his hands, black SWAT clothes, and a rifle slung over his back.

Tears ran down my face. I looked at Buddy and saw him wiping away tears with the back of his hand. I even noticed tears in the eyes of some of the HRT guys.

Then I saw the father. He ran to his family, embracing them all.

The discovery and safe rescue of this family was our Christmas miracle. I couldn't have asked for a better present.

Lastly, the remainder of the team escorted the three men out of the house, each one wearing a pair of handcuffs. Two held their heads down. The third wore a smirk on his face.

Seeing them apprehended was the bow on that Christmas gift.

These perps were put into FBI cars that would take them to an interview room at FBI Headquarters. Once there, the FBI agents would interview them before booking them into the federal prison located in downtown Miami.

Since I was the lead FDLE investigator, and Buddy was the lead FBI investigator on this case, we were both assigned to follow the ambulance transporting the mother and children to the hospital. I needed to speak to Diego, the nine-year-old boy, after the doctor cleared him.

During my interview, I learned a lot. Prior to the kidnapping, when his mother drove him home, he told her his father didn't like the valets to park the Porsche. His mother agreed and parked the car in the garage herself.

As they got out of their car, two men with stun guns attacked them. He and his mother were hit with fists and zapped with the stun guns.

My stomach knotted at the thought of a grown man hitting a little boy with a fist. What kind of cowards were these thugs?

He and his brother and mother were all thrown into the rear of the SUV, covered with blankets to conceal them from anyone in the area, and driven to the house. Once there, they tied Diego's hands together. The man he knew as one of the valets in his condo building watched him to make sure he didn't escape. He kept a television playing, but it had bad reception.

Diego's eyebrows raised. With a sad tone, he said, "He always stopped and told me hi and talked to me when I played on the playground. He was my friend."

He closed his eyes for a moment as if remembering something. "I wasn't allowed to see my mother, but I heard her crying. They gave me McDonalds and donuts to eat."

I asked, "Did the man hurt you besides stunning you and hitting you on your head?"

He looked down. "No."

For some reason, I didn't believe him. I thought that man might have sexually molested him. The way his abductor used the playground to talk with him and befriend him worried me.

If Diego had been the victim of a sexual assault, he wasn't going to admit it. I hoped he wasn't molested.

I arrived home about the time Gary woke up. He poured me a cup of coffee as I briefed him about our great success. We were able to keep this kidnapping from the press and community until the family was rescued.

By early afternoon, Karen and I met to go speak with the kidnapped mother at the condo.

A young, petite woman answered the door in a pair of jeans and a designer blouse that fell loosely over her slender body. Now that I saw her in the daylight, I got to see up close the damage those monsters inflicted upon her. Even her beautiful, long blond hair couldn't distract from her injuries. Black, blue, and green bruises covered her swollen face to the extent that it revealed very little flesh tone.

I had learned that she needed surgery within the next week. The kidnappers had broken her nose and some of the bones around her maxillary-sinus cavity.

Even in her condition, she offered us the traditional Brazilian fruit punch made with two tropical nectars and served in crystal stemmed glasses. She also served guava pastries on a china plate with small linen napkins.

She gave Karen and me the same information Diego had. "The kidnappers seemed surprised I wasn't with my husband when they pulled me out of my car."

I asked, "Did you see any of the kidnappers prior to the incident?"

"Yes, I've seen all of them. They're the valets for our building."

She picked up a pillow on the couch and held it on her abdomen. She then stared out of the picturesque window overlooking the beautiful Atlantic Ocean and appeared deep in thought.

Without taking her eyes off the view, she said, "You know, we chose this penthouse because it seemed so secure. When we were in Brazil, we had armored vehicles and armed guards. We came here to Florida because we thought it'd be much safer."

She squeezed the pillow, still staring at the window. Her tone was flat when she added, "We'll be moving to Fisher Island within a few weeks."

Many famous celebrities lived on Fisher Island, a very exclusive private island paradise. It could only be reached by watercraft or helicopter. A ferry transported vehicles over from the Miami Beach Causeway.

After the interview, Karen and I drove to the FBI building where we learned more about the details surrounding the abduction. The valets turned out to be Venezuelan. The father's business competitor, also Brazilian, offered them fifty thousand dollars to kill the entire family, including the nanny.

The kidnappers had watched and followed the mother and father while they shopped and returned to their neighbor's party. They then went to the underground garage and waited, so they didn't see the nanny and kids walk out the front of the building to the party across the street.

When the Porsche drove into the underground parking area, they thought it contained both the father and the mother. They planned to kill the parents and then lure the nanny and kids out of the penthouse and kill them.

After the kidnappers jumped the mother and son, they realized they had messed up. The dad was the most important person in this scheme. The kidnappers realized entering the alarmed penthouse to get to the father would be difficult. So, plans changed, and they took the mother and kids hostage.

They used the ransom to lure the dad to meet with them. Then they would kill him and the hostages. Greed.

This type of crime shouldn't happen anywhere, but it did. It happened in my country, in the United States of America. It made me angry and offended me.

Thank God for blundering, stupid criminals.

CHAPTER FOUR

MONSTER MOM

Detectives from cold northern states have a tendency to come to South Florida during the winter months. They take advantage of the warm and bright sunshiny days to investigate cases with links to our cities.

I wasn't surprised when Cathy Mueller from the Office of Statewide Prosecution called and told me that Detective Sergeant Raymond Smith, an investigator with the Illinois State Police, had paid her a visit and that he was on his way to my office.

She said, "You'll really like working with him. The case is in your wheelhouse; it's about a child homicide."

I was curious but decided to wait to talk with Detective Smith about the details. I peered outside at the sunny skies, sure he preferred the mild and sunny seventy-eight degrees that our part of the country had to offer over the major snowstorm occurring in Illinois at that time.

After hearing the doorbell ring, I got up to buzz him in. As a small field office, we didn't have a receptionist or gatekeeper, so it was left up to us agents to welcome our guests.

Peering through the glass in the reception area, I admit I was pleasantly surprised at his appearance. His slim frame stood about six feet tall. His brown hair was parted on the side and complemented his boyish face, although the slight crow's feet in the corners of his deep-set brown eyes made me believe he was probably in his early forties.

He saw me as well, pressing his credentials against the glass. I pressed the button that unlocked the door.

I held out my hand to shake his. "Detective Sergeant Smith? I'm Special Agent Floy Turner."

He grinned and took my hand, giving it a firm shake. "Hi, Agent Turner. Thanks for agreeing to meet with me."

I returned his smile. "Sure. I hope I'll be able to help in some way."

What I didn't tell him was how right Cathy was that I would like working with him.

"Follow me." I started walking down the hallway. "Cathy Mueller called and told me you were coming over from her office. How do you know Cathy?"

In my office, I sat behind my desk, and Raymond sat down in the black vinyl chair across from me. "Cathy contacted me a few times over the telephone. That's when she was preparing to prosecute the Back-Door Entry Case involving two of Chicago's finest citizens—Boiko Dolinsky and Donka Lapinski. She had gotten my name and number from a former Chicago police officer. He's retired now and living in Cathy's condominium complex. He had called to tell me that she wanted background information on some of the organized gypsy criminal enterprises out of Chicago.

"So, with this connection, I contacted Miss Mueller." His smile vanished, and his eyes bore into mine. "I'm investigating the cold homicide case of a toddler. My suspect, Dottie Jones, is the victim's mother. She's currently serving fifteen years in the Broward Correctional Institution for the attempted murder of her second child in a Florida case. Cathy told me you had a lot of contacts in the women's prison."

I nodded in confirmation.

He continued. "I wanted to know if you'd be able to help me. It had originally been ruled a SIDS case. The baby was eleven months old and living with her parents in a suburb outside of Chicago when she died."

SIDS, or Sudden Infant Death Syndrome, was a medical term often used by investigators from the medical and criminal fields. They used it to explain how an otherwise-healthy baby under a year old was suddenly found dead inside his or her crib.

This terminology was not used when doctors and criminal investigators determined that an infant's death was the result of a specific interaction by another person. It shouldn't be confused with other similar terms such as shaken-baby syndrome.

Sadly, during my many years in law enforcement, I've encountered situations where people tried to cover up a murder of a baby by yelling SIDS. Good police work usually identified these cowardly acts, so they didn't go unpunished.

Raymond said, "I got a letter from an inmate who's housed in the same prison as Dottie. She says she has some information that Dottie was responsible for murdering her baby."

I forced myself to maintain a poker face. More than likely, this inmate didn't come forward because she was a good citizen. Like most prison inmates, she hoped she would get a favor for her efforts or a transfer to another prison. She might have held a grudge against the inmate she had snitched on, or it could be any combination of all of the above. Whatever the reason, I was curious to learn more.

He moved forward in his chair as if trying to convince me to help him, not that I needed any convincing. He had me at "homicide cold case of a toddler." My heart broke for the senseless tragic death of this baby.

"I'm conducting an in-depth interview of this inmate informant. Her name's Misty Katz. She's a lifer for murdering her husband. I wanted your help in this interview."

"Lifer" is a slang word often used by people involved with the prison system in some fashion, such as law enforcement, wardens, the courts, and inmates. A lifer will never see or breathe the clean air outside the prison walls, and death is the only way out.

I gave a slight smile. "Okay, Raymond. I'll help you."

The big grin spread across his face again. He nodded. "Great. Thank you." His shoulders seemed to relax a bit.

I said, "I suggest we start by visiting your Miss Katz."

Still wearing that same smile, Raymond said, "Let's do it."

His tan slacks and golf shirt made him look more like a regular Floridian or tourist than a cop. However, my navy-blue suit could easily give me away.

"Okay," I said. "Let me change into my blue-collar-worker attire so that I don't alert any of the female prisoners that I'm a cop."

I then went into the ladies' restroom and put on a long-sleeve, light-blue T-shirt, blue jeans, and beige work boots. Of course, I wore my trusty black bandana wrapped around my blond hair. I had adopted this accessory from an FBI agent when we hunted for the dangerous fugitives who had escaped from the Glades Correctional Institution.

We drove from my office to the prison. On the way, I called Broward Correctional Institution (BCI) Inspector Tom Watts. I had known him since my trooper days when my then-partner Jacob and his K-9 Sniffer visited his prison periodically to conduct drug searches. That was when I met Aileen Wournos.

He picked up on the first ring.

"Hi, Tom, this is Floy. I'm about thirty minutes away from you. I'm with a detective for the Illinois State Police, and we need to conduct a covert interview with Misty Katz." I then relayed to him what Raymond had told me.

Too many of the women housed in that prison knew who I was. They couldn't see me speaking with Misty before the investigation even started. Women in prison have a lot of time to just think, sit, and watch. When they observe anything out of the ordinary, including other prisoners who might be snitches, the gossip grapevine grows at Mach One.

Tom said, "Sure, Floy. Do you still have that hardhat from the telephone company?"

"Yes, I do. And I have a tool belt too." The hard hat and my attire were the perfect fit for a utilities worker going into the prison.

Tom said, "Just come to the rear prisoner-transport area. I'll meet you there. I'll then take you both to the medical wing as if the detective's a new caseworker."

When we pulled up, Tom was waiting for us. I introduced him to Raymond and vice versa. He then led us to a small private room to wait for Misty.

Our plan went well. I didn't recognize any inmates during my brief walk to the clinic.

The warden summoned Misty to the medical unit for a routine visit.

A few minutes later, a guard ushered a heavy woman wearing a prison dress into our room. Her round face contained a pale complexion and brown eyes, all of which were framed by shoulder-length brown hair.

She sat down in a plastic chair. Her slightly squinted eyes darted between Raymond and me.

I tried to put her at ease. "Hi, Misty. Thank you for coming. I'm Special Agent Floy Turner with FDLE, and this is Detective Raymond Smith with the Illinois State Police. Detective Smith is here because of the letter you sent regarding Dottie Jones."

Her shoulders and facial muscles relaxed.

I kept my gaze steady. "Misty, I'll get to the point. Would you be comfortable wearing a small recording device for a meeting with Dottie?"

She smiled and answered without hesitation, "Sure." She moved forward in her chair, her eyebrows lifted slightly in what appeared to be excitement.

Raymond and I made sure Misty didn't expect us to promise her any deals as a result of her cooperation. We knew the importance of addressing this issue upfront in case we needed to use Misty's information. We didn't want to jeopardize a future court case should Dottie be tried for the murder of her first child. Dottie's defense could always claim that Misty had pressured Dottie to tell her about the crime so that she could benefit from an assumed deal.

The pitch in Misty's voice was slightly higher, confirming the excitement conveyed by her body language. Prisoners were bored, so just doing something different could give them something to look forward to beyond the mundane. "Dottie told me she smothered her baby Mattie because she thought her husband cared more about the baby than her. She said the baby was evil and that since she was pregnant with her second baby, she wanted to get rid of the first one." She folded her arms before tilting her chin upward. "I hate mothers who hurt their children, and this one murdered hers."

I was sickened by her words, but I refused to show it. I stayed focused and kept to the task at hand. "Misty, do you think you'll be able to get Dottie to admit to killing her baby on tape?"

"Yep," she said with a nod.

Before we went any further, Raymond and I needed to obtain a judicial court order. This would allow us to lawfully record conversations between Misty and Dottie.

In Florida, a sworn law enforcement officer could direct a cooperating witness to wear a covert device for secretly recording a conversation. The tape was used as evidence if the person wearing the wire merely signed a one-party consent form.

However, since this murder occurred in Illinois and would be tried there, we needed to observe Illinois laws. Its wiretap laws were stricter. A court order was needed to surreptitiously obtain a recording of a conversation between two or more parties.

We made arrangements with Tom Watts and Misty to meet the following day to get the recording.

Raymond and I started the drive back to my office for me to write the court order. He was quiet as he stared out the car window.

I put together the court order and took it to the courthouse right afterward for the approval and signature of the on-duty judge. When we entered the courtroom in Broward County to have the order signed, I felt relieved to see Judge Rios from the Goodyear case sitting on the bench.

She looked up and gave a quick smile when she saw me. We waited for almost an hour before the hearing broke for lunch.

She waved us up front to her bench. She smiled and said, "Agent Turner, good to see you again. What do you have for me today?"

I handed her my written order. Her eyebrows furrowed while she read it. "Why do you want a court order for a one-party consent to record?"

"Because if charges are brought against the defendant as part of this investigation, the trial would take place in Illinois."

Judge Rios nodded. She signed the order, and we were good to go.

Upon leaving the courthouse, I called Cathy Mueller. "Hey, we're heading on over to Los Olas Boulevard to grab some dinner and drinks. Want to join us?"

She agreed.

Raymond and I arrived first and asked for a table for three. The hostess took us to an outside table next to the sprawling brick sidewalk.

Raymond still wore his same attire, which included a golf shirt underneath a light jacket. He removed it and hung it on the back of his chair just before sitting down.

Cathy showed up dressed similarly to me. Contrary to Raymond, we were both bundled up in sweaters, scarves, jeans, and boots. I guess we had lived in the tropics for so long that thin blood caused us to freeze when temperatures dropped to sixty-eight degrees. Raymond enjoyed what he thought to be summer weather.

Cathy asked questions about Raymond's investigation. She appeared eager to learn about his next steps going forward.

We told her what had occurred with Misty so far and that we were going back the next day with a wire.

Wired for Sound

The next morning gave us another perfect winter day in South Florida. I woke up early for my morning run. I enjoyed the peaceful blue water as I jogged along an ocean path before coming full circle to my boat.

I proceeded to ready myself for work. Once again, I donned my hardhat and telephone repair outfit before grabbing a cup of java. I then drove to Fort Lauderdale to pick up Raymond at his hotel on 17th Street.

After parking my car, I walked inside the luxurious lobby with a glossy tiled floor. Palm trees and a fountain simulated a tropical environment.

I looked around at the flurry of activity. Many guests looked to be gearing up to leave with their golf bags and fishing gear in tow. I reminded myself that South Florida was experiencing the height of its tourist season.

I spotted Raymond sitting at a table, sipping a cup of coffee. He spotted me too and waved.

On the way to the prison, I called Tom to give him a heads up about our impending arrival. I wanted to make sure he would meet us for our stealth entrance.

We arrived once again near the medical unit and parked. Upon entering the small wing, the smell of antiseptic greeted me. A few prison nurses carried clipboards as they made their rounds, walking from room to room within their quasi-hospital.

Some inmates created mythical illnesses because they knew if they needed medical tests or procedures, they would be sent out of the prison with guards. They considered it a form of personal entertainment. Plus, it gave them a change of environment and something to do to break up their monotonous, routine days.

The warden took Raymond and me to the same small meeting room. When we walked in, I saw Misty already sitting at a gray metal table.

She wore another plain blue-cotton prison-issued dress that showed her unshaven legs. Above her prison-issued sneakers, she wore her prison-issued white socks folded neatly down to her ankles.

We showed her the small, lightweight recording device. I placed it inside her bra between the cups.

I chose this recording device over a wire transmitter. The abundance of steel and concrete inside a prison facility created interference and environmental noise issues. As a result, we would have trouble hearing the conversation.

I said, "Misty, you have to say the time when you begin speaking with Dottie. We need you to get her to tell you how she planned her crime, how she fooled law enforcement and first responders, how and why she committed the murder, and where she committed the murder. We need you to get very specific information that only she, the person who committed this crime, would know. Do you have all of that?"

I searched her face for any signs of hesitation. Instead, she gave a slow smile and raised her right eyebrow. "Yes, Sweetie, I got all of that. No need to worry. I promise to follow all of your directions."

Inside, I breathed a sigh of relief. However, the big one wouldn't be released until we got everything on tape.

Once we turned on the recorder, I conducted the preamble. I gave the place, date, time, as well as my and Raymond's name, rank, and agency. Lastly, I gave them Misty's name and the Department of Correction number for the record.

Misty sauntered out of the room. If she was nervous, she sure didn't show it.

A Chilling Confession Caught on Tape

Raymond and I waited for about two hours. We wished we could hear the conversation as it was happening.

We passed the time by talking about this case, other cases, and our agencies. The whole time in the back of my mind, I hoped and prayed Misty was following through with my instructions, that the tape would be clear, and the entire conversation would be audible.

At last, Misty returned from her recorded meeting with Dottie. That right eyebrow was raised again and along with it, the corners of her mouth. "I got it," she said. "Dottie admitted to killing Mattie and that the murder was premeditated."

I tried not to leap through the air with excitement. Instead, I put on my poker face. "Okay, thanks, Misty. We'll review the recording and get back in touch with you."

After Misty left the room, Raymond and I sat with Tom Watts. The three of us listened to the most chilling recording I have ever heard. I shuddered, feeling as if I had heard the devil himself speak.

The recording was hard to listen to and made me feel sick in my heart to hear how an innocent child could suffer at the hands of her own mother. I have seen and heard a lot of terrible things throughout almost twenty years of my career, but this was the worst. As a mother of two daughters who had brought me so much love and happiness, I couldn't imagine how Dottie could have been so cruel to not one but both of her daughters.

Misty did an excellent job. She used the guise of a Wicca ritual to begin the conversation with Dottie. Wicca is a form of modern pagan religion that incorporates witchcraft. I have heard that this religion had a prison following.

At one point, she told Dottie that they had to tell each other the worst act they had ever committed. Dottie tried to get Misty to go first, but Misty cleverly switched the scenario so that Dottie went first.

When Dottie said, "You already know what I did," Misty didn't miss a beat. She said, "You need to say it again for the cleansing ritual." She encouraged Dottie to relay the gruesome details and say how she murdered her child.

Dottie did. We heard how she treated little Mattie particularly mean. Dottie talked about how little Mattie stood at a glass door looking for her daddy to come home. She described how she practiced smothering her baby with cellophane wrap several times before actually committing the murder.

After killing Mattie, she set the stage over the next fifteen minutes before calling for the ambulance. She wanted it to look like she had been involved with cleaning the dishes, so when the medics arrived, they would assume she had been in the kitchen while the baby was in her crib. She even carried a dish cloth over her shoulder when she went to check on Mattie and soapy water was still in the sink.

My stomach churned.

Misty asked Dottie, "Did you have any remorse after your baby's death?"

Dottie laughed before saying, "I was glad to be finished with the bitch."

I knew if a jury ever heard this recording, they would convict Dottie in a second.

I felt so sad for that baby. When I left the prison, I could barely lift my legs. They felt like weights had been draped around them.

We rode back to Raymond's hotel in stunned silence. Any other time, I would have taken Raymond to dinner and had a victory celebration. Although he got what he wanted, and a little baby was finally going to get the justice she deserved, I didn't feel like celebrating.

I asked, "You okay if I go ahead and take you back to your hotel?"

"Yeah," he responded in a voice barely above a whisper.

Before exiting the car, Raymond turned to me and spoke in a husky voice. "Thanks, Floy, for your help. You know, I wanted to solve this case badly, to get to the truth. Now I have it, and I wish I had never known what she did to her baby."

I nodded but remained silent. I knew exactly what he meant. In fact, he confirmed my feelings.

I drove home with a heavy heart.

<u>Face to Face with the Monster</u>

I arranged to have Dottie moved to another correctional facility. She didn't yet know about the recording, but I wanted her moved to protect Misty.

Dottie was transported to Lowell Prison Annex near Ocala. This was the same prison we stopped at with Aileen Wuornos on the way to the Florida State Prison death chamber.

A few weeks after Misty got Dottie's confession, I picked up Raymond at the Gainesville airport to drive him to the Ocala prison. He had flown in to get an interview with Dottie, and hopefully, her confession. Although we had the tape from her conversation with Misty, a sworn confession to a law enforcement officer would be better for court. It would offer no wiggle room or arguments from the defense since prisoners are known to lie to each other.

Raymond asked, "Did you bring the recording?"

"Yes. I want Dottie to listen to her evil words as she described how she killed her daughter."

When we arrived at Lowell, the warden led us into a small conference room with beige concrete walls, three metal chairs, and a beige metal desk that sat on a gray concrete floor. A small window with bars was the only connection to the outside world.

A correction officer escorted Dottie into the room with us. Since we were in the prison, there was no need for any chains. She wore a blue prison shirt, pants, and white sneakers. Like Misty, she was overweight, the starchy prison food being the probable culprit for the extra pounds. Her short, dirty blonde hair was accentuated by a bad complexion.

She sat down across the gray metal table and looked at us, her face devoid of emotion. Once I pulled out the digital recorder, her face lost all color. I figured she knew what was on it since she was moved to the new prison right after she told Misty her story.

As the tape played, her eyes widened, and her eyebrows were pulled up in the middle with worry.

After we all heard her confession to Misty, Raymond read Dottie her Miranda Rights.

Her first words contained no remorse for her daughter, only for herself. Her voice contained a higher pitch than it did on the tape. "Will I be getting the death penalty?"

Raymond said, "The prosecutor in Illinois said it was possible that if you pled guilty and took a deal, you could receive a life sentence."

She took a deep breath and let it back out. She shrugged. "I'll take life."

If only she considered life for her children.

<u>A Bittersweet Ending</u>

Within a few weeks, Illinois extradited Dottie back to its jurisdiction where she stayed for the next two years. Once her case was settled, and she was sentenced to life in prison for murdering her baby Mattie, she was returned to Florida to finish out her sentence for the attempted murder of her second child.

A couple more years later, she was returned back to Illinois where she would remain behind prison bars for the rest of her life. This truly was a person who should never be allowed to live free in our society.

I returned the favor to Misty. Her girlfriend Inked was incarcerated in Hernando Correctional Institution (HIC). She also seemed to prefer prison dresses just like Misty. However, she had tattoos all over her legs and body. She was thinner than Misty and probably a few years older. She reminded me of Aileen, but she had only been convicted of murdering two of her johns. I arranged for Misty and Inked to be reunited.

Misty and I stayed in contact after this case. Whenever I see an incoming call from a prison, I know Misty is reaching out to me.

Although we received a victory in this case, it contained a very sad footnote. Raymond was killed in a line-of-duty car accident before he got to see Dottie transferred back to Illinois.

He left behind a loving wife and two darling children.

CHAPTER FIVE

HOUSE OF HORRORS

I wanted to be as prepared as possible for my next assignment—investigating computer-based crimes that targeted and victimized children. So, I joined the Law Enforcement Against Child Harm Task Force, also known and referred to as LEACH.

This task force was comprised of federal, state, county, and local law enforcement detectives who specialized in cybercrimes. They focused on computer-based child exploitation.

For predators, the Internet was an effective and more anonymous way to seek out and groom children for criminal purposes, such as producing and distributing child pornography, contacting and stalking children for the purpose of engaging in sexual acts, and exploiting children for sexual tourism for personal and commercial purposes.

Our targets and persons of interest were, of course, pedophiles. These monsters viewed and collected prepubescent pornography for a variety of illegal purposes. Some included private sexual uses, trading with other pedophiles, luring a child into prostitution, and preparing children for sexual abuse. The latter was done through a process called child grooming or enticement. It resulted in sexual exploitation by producing new child pornography.

I drove through the Fort Lauderdale rush-hour traffic to meet Detective Tony Rossi, a fifteen-year veteran with the Broward Sheriff's Office (BSO). I approached the BSO's Undercover Investigations building, marveling at the transformation. Back in the day, this sprawling complex had been a big warehouse with several floors.

I looked around to familiarize myself with my surroundings. As luck would have it, a Starbucks sat across the street, providing a convenient location where I anticipated feeding my caffeine addiction.

A heavy-duty security gate provided the only access to the UC (undercover) building's expansive fenced parking lot. Beautiful tropical landscaping surrounded the area. Although aesthetically pleasing, the large palm trees acted as natural security barriers.

The building itself was even more secure. A red-haired BSO police officer sat behind a desk inside the bullet-proof glass doorway of the vestibule. I flipped open my credentials to show her I was on the job. She stared at them for a moment, looked at me, and then back to my credentials, I guess before realizing I was really the one in the photo on my identification card. A bit annoying, but I appreciated her thorough vetting procedures.

She nodded without smiling and pushed the release lock to allow me entrance. I closed my credentials wallet and placed it back in my pocket.

"Please sign in," she instructed in an emotionless, professional tone.

Either she was not having a good day, or she had the personality of a stick, but I complied nevertheless. I smiled at the officer in hopes of cheering her up. I then bent over the desk and signed my name on the form held by a clipboard.

I looked back at the officer, and she finally returned my smile. So far, so good.

She took the clipboard and pushed three buttons on her black desk phone. "Special Agent Turner is here to see Detective Tony Rossi."

She paused for a moment, looking at me the whole time she listened to whoever was on the other end.

She spoke into the phone again. "Okay, I'll send her on up." She laid the phone back into its cradle. "Agent Turner, down the hallway to the elevators. Second floor. Detective Rossi will be waiting for you."

I gave a quick nod to acknowledge I understood her directions as I pictured them in my mind. She buzzed me through the second locked door.

I walked to the elevators with my mixed emotions now intensified. Although eager to make a difference and protect innocent children, I knew I was about to enter a house of horrors, and what I would see would remain etched in my mind forever.

Chatting with Evil

The elevator doors opened, and a man who looked to be in his mid-forties stood in front of me, smiling. Obviously, he hit the gym constantly because his six-foot frame looked very fit. His neatly cut dark hair surrounded a handsome face punctuated by brown eyes covered by wire-framed glasses, which gave him an intellectual appeal.

"Agent Turner? Tony Rossi." He held out his hand, which I shook. Despite his muscular arms, his handshake was firm but not overpowering.

I immediately liked Tony. His great smile made me feel welcomed.

"I appreciate your working with us," he said. "Before we get started, I'd like to give you the grand tour."

He started down the hall, and I fell in step next to him as he showed me around the four-story building. With the post-9/11 era upon us, flat-screen televisions had been strategically placed everywhere, and the channels were kept on either CNN or FOX.

The multiple conference rooms took on the characteristics of windowless bunkers. TVs and monitors hung on the walls and sat on the banks of desks that also included computers and telephones. These high-tech workstations were reserved for multiple-agency representatives.

The BSO didn't appear to cut any corners with the open squad bays either. I found their state-of-the-art tech equipment and furnishings impressive. In addition to more flat-screen televisions, sleek desks with faux-leather swivel computer chairs rested upon attractive deep-blue and green carpet. Overall, the décor seemed appropriate and not too flashy.

The atmosphere contained a high level of testosterone. Most of the task force members came from local, county, state, and federal law enforcement agencies, and they all seemed to take the term "staying fit" seriously. I appreciated this opportunity to be around theses buffed-macho deputies, detectives, and special agents located under one roof.

We continued down the hallway until we came to a closed door. After swiping his ID card over the sensor, he led me into the secured room assigned to this task force. A row of a half-dozen computers sat on top of desks, down the length of the room. Only undercover detectives used these computers to obtain evidential images of children being sexually exploited and/or molested.

These cases were not for the faint at heart. I knew those computer screens held images of some of the worst child abuse that were transmitted around the world through the Internet. A normal person couldn't even imagine the extent of depravity.

Tony tilted his head toward a computer that had an empty chair in front of it. "Go ahead and sit down at that computer. You're going to need to create a profile."

I complied and logged on for the first time with my new user name and password. Next, I followed Tony's directions and clicked onto a chat site called "Daddies Looking for Young Girls."

I created a profile. Using the Internet name Cherie, I made myself thirteen years old with long blond hair, five feet six inches tall, and weighing one hundred ten pounds. I loved to surf and hang out near the beach. My parents didn't understand me. They were control freaks who wouldn't let me go to the mall alone. I loved dogs, video games, lip gloss, and shopping. I kept to myself and didn't have a best friend. The boys at my school were all jerks. School was boring.

In truth, I had no idea what thirteen-year-old kids did these days. My kids were grown and gone.

Regardless, within thirty seconds, I received five responses wanting to "chat." They asked my age, or I confirmed it, and I told them what my hobbies were.

I really didn't know who was talking with me. These responders could have been male, female, young, or old. However, past criminal investigations all indicated that these faceless child predators were mostly men. They engaged in this activity for pleasure and profit.

This happened to be my first experience with these types of perverts. I witnessed how tenacious they were in scoring with a child they met online through the convenience of instant messaging (IM). They usually started a few conversations, and then they expressed a desire to meet at a mall or other public venue.

Not five minutes had passed when I got a couple of possibilities online looking to meet me. These sickos disgusted me. I knew they were trolling for innocent children to lure into their webs of perverted sex.

They also requested a picture from Cherie, so I realized I needed a picture for my fake online profile. I considered using my own childhood pictures. Hurricane Andrew had destroyed many of them, and those I did find looked too dated. So, I asked a young female law enforcement officer who worked in the undercover office if she could give me one.

To get myself up to speed with the IMs, I had to learn another language. IMs use computer slang. My first slang term, "P911" or "PA," are known as *parent alert*. These abbreviations are used in situations where a parent attempts to look over your shoulder during a chat. If I didn't reply quick enough, my responders asked "AYST," which translated to "Are you still there?"

I thought the perverts in the rest areas where I worked undercover as a prostitute during my trooper days were a sick, slimy bunch. However, they had nothing on these Internet perverts.

When working these cases, we subpoenaed the Internet Protocol (IP) address from the chatter's screen name. We then set up a meet, which proved to be the best way to snag these guys. Because they would travel from other cities and states to hook up with the "perfect child" from online, we referred to them as "travelers."

I must say that Tony made a much better teenage girl than me. I enjoyed watching his chats when he portrayed himself as Janey, a fifteen-year-old cheerleader. The thought that the perv on the other end had no idea that Tony had a five-o'clock shadow came across as too funny. For me, fooling the perv with Tony's facade turned out to be the fun part of working cybercrimes.

Tony was the best when messaging and making a date with a fifty-year-old man, and he carried on similar conversations with male chatters from all walks of life.

One in particular was a church choir member. The perv instigated a plan to show up at a city park near Janey's school to engage in sex. Parks were common meeting places.

Tony agreed to meet the choir member. He then asked, "What will you bring me?"

Perv said, "How about a stuffed animal?"

Tony, aka Janey, said, "I love horses."

The real fun now began for me. Tony and I were assigned to the arrest team, so I got to "cuff and stuff" these guys into the car for transporting. I always did it with a big smile on my face.

Tony and I arrived early so we could get in position and hide nearby on our stomachs behind the wooded vegetation in the park.

For our decoy, we chose a trim, blonde twenty-something officer who looked like a teenager. She always kept her back to the predator as she sat atop a picnic table under a pavilion.

When the meet time arrived, I watched a slightly overweight, middle-aged man wearing jeans and a button-down white shirt approach our decoy. He was easy to spot and identify because of the yellow stuffed horse he carried.

My adrenaline pumped as I picked myself up off the ground and ran up with the rest of our team with our weapons drawn.

I yelled, "Police! Drop the bag and put your hands in the air."

Perv stopped and threw both hands in the air, dropping everything he had been carrying. I holstered my gun and ran over to him. I then got the pleasure of placing my handcuffs around his wrists.

He offered no resistance but did say, "I just wanted to meet her and talk with her. Nothing else. I swear. I would never hurt a child."

Tony searched him and found condoms and lubricant in his pockets, common items that pervs concealed on their person or in the bag with the gifts. He also found some taffy candy.

In another case, a retired Army Colonel traveled from Ohio to Florida to meet and have sex with Janey. He deviated from the normal meeting place by checking into a high-end hotel where he arranged for Janey to meet him.

When the meeting time arrived, our undercover "teenage" cop walked to the room number and knocked on the door. She then turned around so her back would be to the perv.

Those of us on the takedown team stood against the hallway walls on each side of the door, making sure we were out of sight from the peephole's view. When the colonel opened it for Janey, she stepped aside so we could enter his room and arrest him.

His eyes widened in shock before darting around the room to glance at each of us. We searched his person and personal items, looking for the condoms and lubricant. We located them under the mattress. I found it pitiful but so rewarding to catch these guys before they could commit this type of crime on young victims.

Cases such as these resulted in the conviction of many traveler suspects, usually through a plea bargain. They received long prison sentences. Very few of these crimes went to trial. These guys didn't want the publicity about their activity.

I couldn't blame them.

<u>Sugar Daddy</u>

Once we identified the IP addresses of local online chatters and pornography traders, we conducted surveillance to verify the actual location and user on the computer. On several occasions, Tony, a.k.a. Janey, was back as the undercover officer on the computer with the chatter.

I would go with other task force members to the house of the suspect's computer. I would knock on the door and speak with the person who answered. My role was to play the part of a new neighbor looking for her lost dog. I even carried a dog leash as my prop.

My mission was to place the bad guy on the computer. Even though we would be able to get a warrant either way, the case would be easier to prove with his statement acknowledging he was on the computer or the only one at home.

I would say, "I hope I haven't interrupted you, but I'm new in the neighborhood. I'm looking for my dog that just ran off."

If the person at the door said, "No problem, I was on my computer," then I had just lucked out. This did happen a few times.

If this didn't happen, I asked, "Is anyone else at home who might have seen my dog?"

If the door answerer said, "I'm the only one here," then bingo! We completed our mission. I could testify that he had said he was the only one home. Therefore, he must have been the person on the computer. I would leave, but I would come back, usually the next day or as soon as a judge signed the search warrant. This time, though, my gun and handcuffs replaced the leash.

On the other hand, if more than one person was home, then I would attempt to engage him in a conversation. I would ask, "Could you bring anyone else who's home to the door so that I can describe my dog to them? See if maybe they've seen Buddy?"

One cool evening in the fall, as Tony and I prepared to leave the office, we received information from a uniformed patrol officer. He had been on the scene of an attempted child abduction. A fourteen-year-old boy had been in a chat room on the computer with a possible suspect.

We headed out to the address in Margate. Upon arriving, we saw a BSO patrol car parked in front of an older, brown concrete-block house. We entered the home and saw the responding officer standing in a small living room next to a kid and a woman sitting on a couch.

The boy's eyebrows were pulled up in the middle, and he was visibly shaking. He was small for his age. He kept pushing the bangs of his shaggy dark-blonde hair out of his eyes. I wasn't sure if it was because he wanted to see better or if he was nervous.

The cop introduced himself to us. He then said, "This here's Craig Smith and his mother Patty. Craig told me he had been exploring chat rooms where gay men chatted and started chatting to someone by the name of Sugar Daddy."

The boy tilted his head up to us. "I just wanted to check out some of these sites." He looked down and murmured, "I'm just not sure whether I'm straight or gay."

I leaned my head to the side to try to see his eyes better.

When he raised his face back up, I saw a tear on his cheek. He said, "I told him where I went to school and where I lived. I told him I'd meet him, but then I changed my mind."

He looked around at us, his wide eyes pleading for understanding. "I got off the bus this afternoon and saw a man who looked like Sugar Daddy. I started walking home, and he followed me in a blue Chevrolet. When I got to my house, he got out of his car and called my name. I freaked out and ran inside. That's when I called you." He looked back down.

I asked, "Was anyone else here?"

"No. My mom was at work, and my dad doesn't live here. I called my mom, and she came home."

I glanced at the mother. She held her fidgeting hands in her lap. Her eyes pleaded with me for help.

I said, "We're going to need to take your computer."

He nodded without looking up.

We seized the boy's computer but discovered no incriminating evidence. This youngster learned a valuable lesson to never divulge personal information over a computer to a person you don't know.

The Nicest Guy in the Neighborhood

A few weeks later, Tony and I traveled to a neighborhood in Plantation on another case. We were armed with a search warrant for a thirty-year-old man who traded child pornography online.

When we arrived at the suspect's home, an elderly woman, who looked to be in her mid-eighties, opened the door. When she stood, she slumped forward as if she was too weak to stand. She wore a pink turban on her head, and she didn't have any eyebrows or eyelashes.

I assumed she was undergoing chemotherapy. I felt terrible for her and that a member of her family was indulging in this appalling act in her home.

I softly said, "Ma'am, we have a warrant to search your house. We'll need to search any and all computers in the home as well as look at all video tapes and pictures."

Her eyebrows furrowed, and she started to visibly shake. I'm sure she was afraid. Combine that with her illness, and my heart went out to her.

"Why? I don't understand why you would want to search my home."

I stepped inside. "Ma'am, let me get you some water." I took her gently by the arm and led her to the couch. "Here, please sit down."

She complied and hung her head. I went into the kitchen to get a glass of water for her. When I returned, her head was still hung down.

I asked, "Do you live here alone?"

She didn't lift her head. Her voice sounded weak. "No. My grandson lives with me. He's such a good boy for helping me out."

I didn't respond. Instead, I turned around and squeezed my eyes shut. When I turned back around, she was still in the same position.

I asked, "Is your grandson home?"

"No, but he will be soon."

"Can you tell me where his room is?"

She murmured, "Down the hall. Last door on the right."

"Thank you." I started to walk away when the front door opened.

A middle-aged, nice-looking, clean-cut guy stood in the doorway. He looked around with a smile on his face. "What's going on here?"

Tony walked over to him. "Detective Rossi. Sir, we have a warrant to search your home, all computers, videos, and pictures. We'll need you to take a seat over there." Tony pointed to a recliner in the living room. "First, we're going to have to pat you down for our safety. Do you have any weapons?"

Grandma's good boy remained calm as he continued to smile. "I understand. No weapons."

He watched Tony while being searched.

I asked him, "Do you live here?"

"Yes."

"What kind of work do you do?"

He glanced up. "I'm a photographer for little-league football in the fall and a church camp counselor in the summer."

I thought, *Both of these venues give you great opportunities to develop a target-rich environment.*

Once Tony finished his search of good boy, I went to help our technical agent with the search of the house. Tony stayed in the living room with the grandmother and our suspect.

When I entered good boy's bedroom, the framed pictures of prepubescent boys on his walls first caught my attention. A collection of video games sat on his desk. When I searched his closet, I found it full of the types of DVD movies that appealed to children.

However, the video recorder mounted to a doorframe alarmed me the most. It worried me that he may have lured young boys into this room and recorded them.

On his desk sat a computer that was turned off. The tech began the process of removing the computer and any equipment attached to it.

Our task force stayed busy. One detective video-taped the home while another drew a diagram of the house and created an inventory receipt of all the evidence gathered.

In the meantime, Tony sat on the sofa speaking with the man. He used compassion, understanding, and sympathy as techniques to draw a confession from the suspect during the interview.

When interviewing sex offenders, detectives must be soft with their approach or even shift the blame to the victim. Through my experiences in interviewing suspects of crimes against children, I realized the importance of not acting shocked or disgusted by any admission from the culprit.

Many times when trying to get a confession from a pedophile, I would tell him, "I understand how that three-year-old kept crawling into your lap. She just wouldn't let you alone."

We had to stay focused on reaching our goal of obtaining that all-important confession to be used as evidence in trial.

Tony was a pro and obviously used all the right techniques. They worked. This man gave it up.

He stayed relaxed and never showed a sign of nervousness. "Yep, yep, I have a problem. I admit I'm drawn to young boys. I like looking at sexual pictures of them on my computer. I guess you could say I might have done some things that could be construed as inappropriate… even sexually… to several of the boys I had a chance to interact with."

Our search led to the confiscation of his computer, numerous video tapes and DVDs, and a video camera. After we finished with the house, we booked this man into the county jail.

The next evening, we conducted a neighborhood canvass to learn more about this guy's interactions with the neighborhood children. Every neighbor we spoke to proclaimed him to be the nicest guy in the neighborhood. They all gave examples of his friendliness and helpfulness.

Unfortunately, we learned that some of the neighborhood children did fall victim to this predator. We went through the discovered tapes, and our suspicions were confirmed as to why that video recorder was attached to the wall. He had been raping young boys in his bedroom and taping it. He then uploaded these videos on the Internet, sharing them with other pedophiles.

One of his victims was the son of a police officer. None of this surprised me. Some of the traits I've observed in these predators include their abilities to be cunning and manipulative to achieve their goals, and the children of police officers can be just as vulnerable to these tactics.

<u>When Protector Becomes Predator</u>

On the flip side, Tony and I investigated a case that involved a police officer who happened to be the bad guy.

When we identified the house where the trading of child pornography took place through the IP address, we saw a marked police car parked in the driveway. I felt weird following this cop in his car and watching his house, even if it was only for a day.

Tony and I contacted that police department's internal affairs (IA) division. We notified them of our investigative efforts of one of their officers. A detective from IA joined us for the remainder of this investigation. We worked well together.

We had no choice; we knew we would have to arrest him. All of us were sickened to know that a protector had become a predator. In this case, the predator pretended to be a protector.

I actually knew this police officer. I saw him in the Liberty City substation when I worked the Robbery Interdiction Detail (RID) as an FDLE special agent. He was a sergeant with more than twenty-five years on the force.

I was relieved to learn that IA had arranged for a police psychologist to join us when we arrested the sergeant in case the situation went south. It was a preventive measure to protect the suspect should he become suicidal.

As a police officer, arresting one of your own is always difficult. This wasn't Tony's first time; he had arrested two other police officers prior to my assignment with LEACH. Both had committed suicide while out on bond awaiting trial.

Before going to the officer's house, we needed to consider a few possibilities. We knew his girlfriend lived with him. She worked as a clerk at a nearby gas station. Her seventeen-year-old daughter also lived with them. We didn't know if they would be there. If they were, I was assigned to interview both of them while the task force searched the residence.

We also had to consider a serious obstacle that often arose when dealing with police officers who were criminal suspects. We needed to make sure that when we entered his house with the search warrant, he wasn't armed.

To accomplish this feat, someone decided that I would use the lost dog trick. I don't remember taking part in making this plan. I wondered if Tony considered me dispensable, or perhaps he believed in my undercover abilities so much that he knew I could get the fox out of his lair.

According to the plan, once I got him outside, a hidden takedown team would arrest him. We all hoped he didn't have a gun hidden under his clothes.

The plan went off without a hitch. The officer must have really been into dogs. He offered to help me look throughout the neighborhood.

The task force burst into the house. A thin woman came scurrying out of the kitchen to see what had just happened. When she saw six armed strangers wearing bulletproof vests in her living room and handcuffing her boyfriend, her eyes opened wide while her mouth fell open.

I asked her in a gentle yet firm tone, "Are you Sandy?"

Her wide eyes made their way to my face. She nodded.

"Is there somewhere we can go to talk?"

She stood as if paralyzed. I assumed she was numb with fear. After a couple of moments, she turned to go back to the kitchen. I followed.

She sat at the wooden kitchen table and stared straight ahead. Her eyes darted from me to the wall. At this point, they were the only part of her skeletal body that moved.

At first, I thought Sandy had to be in her late fifties. After talking with her, I learned that she was only in her early forties. The wrinkles obtained from too much sun and too many cigarettes compounded her premature aging. Her unkempt head of long blond locks of hair fell from gray roots. She wore dirty shorts and a stained T-shirt. Her bare feet revealed long and dirty toenails.

Frankly, Sandy's appearance floored me. I had only seen the officer extremely well-groomed. He seemed to always wear a spotless pressed uniform, shined shoes, and a close-cut military-style haircut with each black hair in place.

Sandy asked, "Will they search the garage?"

"Yes. We're searching every place in the house."

Her face appeared to whiten even more.

I asked, "Why are you worried about the garage?"

"Will I go to jail if you find my weed?"

"Not if you come clean and tell me where it is, what's been going on in this house, and about your relationship with the officer."

Sandy nodded and took in a deep breath. "I hide a stash of marijuana in a coffee can in the garage. He wouldn't like me smoking pot, so I've got to hide it from him and smoke it in the backyard after he leaves for work."

I thought about the hypocrisy of this man. He had committed such horrific crimes day in and day out, yet he condemned this poor woman for sneaking around with her misdemeanor pot-smoking crime. As a cop, he had to have known she smoked weed.

Sandy's eyes widened as she confirmed my thoughts. "He's very controlling. I've got to account for how I spend every minute of my day. I don't have any friends. He only allows me to go to the gas station where I work as a clerk."

Although she seemed more relaxed, I could still sense the fear. She stared down at the table as she continued to speak. "He gets home late in the afternoons. The first thing he does is lock himself in his computer room. I'm not allowed to go in there. He keeps it locked all the time."

She briefly met my gaze before looking down again. I saw tears in her eyes. "I caught him spying on my daughter when she was taking a shower. One time when she was taking a bath, I caught him lying on the floor in the hallway trying to look under the bathroom door. Ever since then, he doesn't hang around the bathroom anymore when my daughter's in there."

I later discovered why he no longer hung around the bathroom. I found a video recorder hidden inside a clock kept on the bathroom counter. This pervert sat in his locked computer room and viewed this teenager in the bathroom.

Sandy lived with this creep for twelve years. Her possessions consisted of an old, rusted, banged-up camper pickup truck and nothing else.

In my opinion, this officer probably chose Sandy as a life-mate so that he could gain access to her daughter. This is a common trait for pedophiles. They often find a significant other, but their hidden agenda excluded love and companionship with that person. Instead, they want to exploit and molest their children.

We confiscated the officer's pornography, which turned out to be the largest collection I had ever seen. It contained disgusting images of so many innocent victims. They qualified as the worst of the worst.

Tony and I spent weeks sitting in a secured conference room taking copious notes for our investigative summary to give to the prosecutor. What he had in his collection was so disturbing that viewing them shook us to the core. Some nights we didn't want to go straight home, so we decided to go out and have a drink just to unwind. We couldn't share these images with anyone, not even our spouses. This was the hardest part of working crimes against children and keeping yourself mentally healthy.

Along the way, I came across the seized videos of Sandy's daughter in the bathroom. I discovered that he videotaped some of the daughter's school friends when they visited the house. We had to identify these victims and notify their parents. Telling the parents was hard. Naturally, they were horrified. They thought their daughters would be safe visiting the home of a police officer. The child victims had no idea what had happened.

The charges for the prosecution kept mounting.

This officer never again resided in the free world. He will spend the rest of his life behind bars. He wasn't fit to be a member of society, let alone a police officer.

The daughter received some counseling, but Sandy could no longer live in the officer's house. She still had her daughter, her job, and her truck, but no financial security. Still, I hope she's happier now that she's been freed from this monster.

A Ghost from the Past Reappears

Only those who have walked in our shoes and viewed the horrific things done to children could understand this journey.

All of the LEACH task force members were required to visit a shrink on an annual basis. This administrative order must have come through the chain of command by a well-intentioned non-police person. Evidently, this person had some authority within the hierarchy of the department.

Every time I was forced to sit on the couch, I thought I was better grounded than the psychologist, but then maybe every crazy person shares that same opinion. I know I acquired and maintained my mental well-being through my faith and a determination to protect the victims.

It helped when task force members let off steam together. We thoroughly enjoyed getting together with the gang for a few drinks at the local cop bar.

All of us took our assignment to help kids seriously, but not at the expense of our families. Both Tony and I were committed to our spouses and possessed strong moral foundations.

A few weeks after finishing the "cop case," Tony rushed into my cubicle at the LEACH office. "Floy, would you write a search warrant for us to take to a judge to sign?"

He set his case file in front of me and opened it. Leaning over his papers, he began to highlight those items that needed to be included in the warrant.

I knew the warrant involved child porn, so I typed away as I reviewed the contents of his case file.

An undercover detective in Orlando had been working a covert sting through an Internet site. The UC played the role of a father selling his thirteen-year-old virgin daughter. He got a buyer, and they agreed to meet at a restaurant parking lot in Orlando where this perv could pay the father cash to have sex with his child.

The operation turned out to be a success. The perv drove all the way to Orlando to have sex with a minor, and now he was in jail for his efforts.

The UC needed a search warrant for the suspect's house to seize his computer, which was electronic evidence. He didn't have jurisdiction in Broward County where the suspect lived, so he came to Tony for assistance.

A couple of times, I typed in the name Laura Boyer. My brain functioned on automatic, focusing on Tony's case. But something in my mind clicked as I typed Laura's name for the third time.

Laura Boyer was the friend of Sally Goodyear, the mother of little Nancy. I had investigated Nancy's cold-case murder a few years back, but I couldn't gather the evidence the prosecutor needed to take it to trial.

During that investigation, I never could locate Laura for an interview. The night before Nancy's abduction and murder ten years ago, Laura was at Nancy's house with her parents.

The possibility intrigued me. Was she the same Laura Boyer?

I became excited as I wrote the search warrant for her house. Laura's husband was the same perv arrested earlier that morning in Orlando for wanting to purchase the thirteen-year-old virgin from the UC. Small world.

As I looked further through the case file, I discovered that Laura's husband had garnered a significant criminal history. For instance, he had served twenty years in an Ohio prison for homicide.

I called Karen Kool from the FBI, since she had worked with me on the Goodyear case. I invited her to take part in this long-awaited interview of Laura.

Karen said, "I'll come by your office, and we can ride together to Laura's house."

I finished the search warrant, ate a power bar, and drove to the courthouse where I obtained the on-call judge's signature. I returned to my office and found Karen waiting for me.

Tony, Karen, and I climbed into Tony's car to drive to Laura's house. I sat in the backseat, pondering what I would say to Laura.

I asked, "Tony, I assume Mrs. Boyer knows her husband's been arrested?"

Tony turned his head slightly to answer me while still keeping his eyes on the road. "Oh, yeah, she knows. Hubby called her from jail."

I nodded and pondered more.

When I knocked on Laura's door, a buxom woman opened it holding a baby on her hip, who looked about a year old. I couldn't see any resemblance with her mother. Her wispy, light blond hair, blue eyes, and rosebud mouth contradicted Laura's long, light-brown hair, freckles, and green eyes.

Laura's lips parted slightly when she saw the three of us standing at her door with a warrant. Her lips then turned into a frown while her eyebrows lowered between rapidly blinking eyes. She shook her head, her lips now pursed. "That sick son of a bitch is cursed by his sex drive."

I asked, "Laura Boyer?"

She took in a deep breath and rolled her eyes.

I wanted to start off with a non-threatening question to dispel any hostility she may have about the warrant. I had been looking for her for so long, and I wanted her to talk with me.

"I'm Special Agent Turner." I motioned to Tony and Karen. "These are Detective Rossi and Special Agent Kool. Do you know Sally Goodyear?"

Her eyes opened wide as her head jerked backward. "Sally Goodyear. Wow, that was a lifetime ago. I can't believe you're asking about her after all these years."

I looked at her darling baby girl. She smelled like dirty diapers and looked filthy. In addition, she looked small and frail for her age, as if she could be a victim of a failure-to-thrive child-abuse case.

Maybe Laura wasn't providing the proper nutrition for her child. The welfare of this little girl concerned me.

I thought Laura's chaos probably occurred from her own poor judgment. Her history was anything but encouraging. She had hung with the Goodyears, who drank a lot and did drugs. Now she's with her child's father, who was a sicko pervert and also did time for murder. History seemed to be repeating itself.

I said, "We have a warrant to search your home. Because your husband was arrested for soliciting sex from a minor, we're investigating a crime that involves the Internet and a child."

I couldn't catch the words she murmured under her breath.

Laura glanced at the warrant and opened the door wider, stepping aside to allow our entrance.

When we walked into the house, I observed how its messy condition reflected Laura's chaos. In the refrigerator I saw only a lot of beer but no milk. In fact, I didn't see any appropriate food for the baby.

I asked, "Did you know your husband served time for murder?"

"Yes, I knew that. He's actually an okay guy. He just made some mistakes."

We seized her husband's computer, CDs, and DVDs. We examined the bedroom that held her husband's desk. Tony discovered a hidden camera in the corner of the ceiling near a window.

I thought, *All of these guys are recording.*

Well, it was evidence. Just because he was a pedophile did not preclude him from other strange sexual encounters; he just preferred sex with children. The camera and recordings might have illegal activities. For all we knew, he could have had kids in the bedroom when his wife was away or maybe molested their child.

We traced the wire into the laundry room and up the wall. Tony climbed onto the older-model washing machine. He then pushed up the tile of the drop ceiling and exposed a video recorder.

I walked out to the back porch where Laura sat with her baby. "Laura, will you please come with me to the laundry room?"

She stood up and walked in front of me. I showed her the video and explained the camera was focused on her bed. She went ballistic. A string of obscenities continued to flow out of her mouth.

Once Laura cooled down, Karen and I took her to the living room where we suggested she sit.

She leaned her head back and stared at the ceiling. "Well, now that my meal ticket's going to prison for a while, guess I'll need to go back to stripping."

From what I've seen when investigations took me into strip clubs was that the dayshift dancers look better with their clothes on. This unappealing thought opened the door for me to ask her about the Goodyear case. "We need to talk to you about Nancy Goodyear. I could never locate any records for where you lived or worked. Where have you been?"

"I moved to Atlanta where I worked in gentlemen's clubs and the streets until I married and moved back to Florida."

Karen asked, "What happened that day when Nancy went missing?"

Laura told us about the swimming pool incident where she and Sally were engaging in girl sex when Sally's husband Dan caught them. She explained how angry he became when they refused to let him join them. Her account mirrored what Sally Goodyear had told us when we were investigating little Nancy's murder.

Karen asked, "Do you have *any* knowledge about who might have killed Nancy?"

Laura shook her head. "No."

We continued to ask more questions. Laura could have more information and not have realized it was important.

It soon became apparent she didn't have anything new to tell us, so the conversation shifted. At least she verified what we knew about the pool incident and the possibility that Dan might have gotten so angry he went over the edge and killed little Nancy.

What she did know was that she didn't like Dan Goodyear. "Dan is one mean son-of-a-bitch," she said.

Laura shifted the baby to her other side. "The Department of Children and Families is after my ass for child neglect. Can you put in a good word for me?"

I promised Laura I would be in touch with DCF. However, I didn't tell her what I would say to them.

Things didn't turn out well for Laura. Her husband's computer revealed his deal to buy a child for five hundred dollars. It gave us the evidence we needed to make sure he was put away for a long time. He was subsequently convicted of child sex trafficking.

Laura also lost custody of her child. She relocated to Tampa and continued to call me on and off for a year. She kept wanting me to put in a good word for her with DCF.

That wasn't going to happen.

A Dangerous Sex Offender

The Department of Justice (DOJ) honored me with an invitation to attend the first National Human-Trafficking Conference on July 16, 2004, in Tampa. They even promised to have an unannounced special speaker.

The DOJ also requested that I not bring a gun while attending the conference, which created a potential conflict. According to FDLE policy, anytime I was on duty in the state of Florida, I was required to be armed.

To compromise, I decided to take my guns anyway, but I kept them locked in a safe in my car's trunk.

With my clothes packed, I planned to drive to Tampa the day before the conference began. Then the LEACH supervisor called and said he needed me for a search warrant and an arrest warrant, which meant I had to postpone my plans. Admittedly, I felt disappointed.

I left the unbearable heat behind as I entered the coolness offered by the UC building. Upon walking into the LEACH conference room, I saw Tony. I sat next to him while another LEACH task force member briefed us on the details of a child porn case and the suspects who weren't new to law enforcement. He then requested assistance with the warrants.

I recognized one of the names—Donald Timbers. Karen Kool had told me about a life-threatening fight she and a Fort Lauderdale detective got into with Timbers when she was a member of the LEACH Task Force prior to 9/11. The detective had to have surgery after Donald beat him badly. Karen received a black eye and a sprained wrist. Despite their injuries, they continued to fight with everything in them; it was a matter of life and death. Somehow, Karen managed to handcuff Donald during this confrontation.

I grabbed my cell phone and stepped outside to call Karen. She answered after a few rings and confirmed Timbers as the one she arrested.

She said, "He served over four years in prison, but he was recently released. He's now on federal probation."

I said, "I'll make sure the task force members know about Timbers. I'll keep you in the loop on this case."

After returning to the meeting, I raised my hand to speak. I told everyone about Timbers' violent history with law enforcement. Tony and I both commented that we needed SWAT to make the entry on this case.

The commander made the decision to include SWAT from BSO. They were some of the best in the business.

Because SWAT couldn't come to the UC building due to the uniforms and SWAT truck, the LEACH members met them at a staging area in the rear of a large shopping center near Timbers' house. A second briefing was conducted there, and then we lined up the vehicles before responding to the target location.

This commander told the SWAT commander, whom he outranked, to direct SWAT to dress down for the warrant raid. I didn't understand his logic. This order went against SWAT protocol.

In my experience, SWAT involved a specialized strategy and training for response. The members were at great risk and practiced in full gear, including heavy body armor, ballistic shields, motion detectors, assault rifles, and other types of weapons. They knew a proper, well-rehearsed response would allow them to be prepared at all times.

All these preparations eliminated some of the danger for the SWAT members as well as the suspects they would attempt to capture. Since their training was so specialized and encompassed known safety tactics, only a SWAT supervisor should evaluate a situation to make changes for the known best practices.

The team complied, but I noticed how mad they seemed as they opened their car trunks and tailgates. They cursed as they took off their SWAT tactical gear and changed into T-shirts and jeans right there in the parking lot.

We arrived at Timbers' home, a one-story dirty-white ranch style built in the sixties. A chain-link fence surrounded the yard. A few large trees provided a wealth of shade from the hot Florida sun.

A concrete parking pad extended from the front of the house. We walked through a recessed doorway before knocking on a faded-green wooden door to serve Timbers the warrants. No one answered, leaving us to assume that no one was at home.

The lack of response also left us to improvise our entrance. We opened the door with a rammer and crowbar.

The inside of the home mirrored the outside with dirty white-tiled floors and dingy and smudged white walls. Threadbare, holey drapes complemented the worn mismatched furniture. A horrible odor made the whole house smell like roadkill that even buzzards wouldn't touch.

The only sign of life was two large, docile, black-and-tan long-haired dogs standing to the side. Both dogs held their ears back and tucked their tails down between their hind legs. They allowed me to pet them as I tried to comfort them with treats I discovered in the kitchen. One of the dogs then ran into a closet and refused to leave.

We were able to seize a computer in our search, but that was it. Although disappointing, we did experience one success. While we searched the house, another LEACH member patrolled the area and spotted Timbers driving home about a block away and arrested him for possession of child pornography.

I left mentally exhausted, tired, and dirty for my five-hour drive across the state to Tampa to attend the human-trafficking conference.

When I reached Tampa at eleven that night, I pulled into the beautiful Marriott Hotel on the water. I self-parked, leaving my shotgun and AR-15 in a gun locker in my trunk. I knew I would feel naked if I went inside to the conference without being somewhat armed, so I decided to sneak in my smaller weapons. I put my Glock and my Smith and Wesson in my large purse and walked into the luxurious lobby.

Fortunately, the conference wasn't starting until the morning because I still felt dirty and stinky. I had to walk through the lobby to check in, so I wore jeans with a clean suit jacket to cover the sweat and dirt that had collected on my pullover shirt. My hair, however, still smelled like those old dogs.

I noticed many Secret Service agents walking around the lobby. Cops can usually spot the Secret Service agents attending an event where the POTUS (President of the United States) may appear. They were typically the best-dressed and best-groomed folks there. Plus, they always talked into their coat sleeves.

Then it hit me like a ton of bricks. I suddenly understood why I couldn't wear a sidearm into the conference. President George W. Bush was the unannounced keynote speaker!

I scurried up to my room. When I entered, my jaw dropped. A beautiful view of the marina clearly seen through my oversized windows greeted me. Furthermore, my room turned out to be a suite of two rooms for one tired gal.

I soaked in the tub and watched television. When hunger overcame me, I dove into the honor bar in my room. I indulged in a bag of cashews and four mini-bottles of red wine. Exhaustion left me too tired to even go down and see who might be at the bar.

Thankfully, I had packed a good suit, a pretty blouse, and fashionable accessories that would come in handy now that I would be mingling with those good-looking Secret Service agents. I was glad I didn't need to talk into my coat sleeve all day.

The next morning, I locked my remaining guns in my FDLE car. I then went through the security check to attend the opening ceremony.

This was the Department of Justice's first-ever training on human trafficking. President Bush felt strongly about being involved with the kick off for this deplorable crime.

This conference became a turning point for me. Not only did it redirect my focus on human trafficking, but it introduced me to those who were going to be experts in the field in Florida.

I formed bonds with some of the attendees I had known from Miami and Florida's west coast. These friendships remained strong because some of us have collaborated for decades about combating human trafficking.

A Search Warrant Gone Really Bad

Two months after the conference, I was deployed to Port Charlotte on Florida's southwest coast because of Hurricane Charley. This storm created severe damage there. Gary and his squad from the Palm Beach field office were also deployed there.

Port Charlotte's motels and hotels were badly damaged, so we had to attend a briefing on our hurricane-duty assignments in the Fort Myer's FDLE office, which was forty-three miles away. While waiting for the meeting to start, I sipped coffee in the conference room and watched television. The breaking news reported a police officer-involved shooting in Fort Lauderdale.

It then showed a dirty white house that I recognized as Timbers'. The reporter said one officer was dead and another wounded.

I picked up a landline and called Tony. When he spoke, his voice broke up. He said, "While you were deployed, and Timbers was in jail, he and his boyfriend kept talking on the phone about how the police missed hidden evidence in their house during the first search. Once we heard this, we got the second warrant."

Tony went on to tell me that a dozen LEACH detectives went to Timbers' house. When they entered it to execute the warrant, the boyfriend was waiting for them. He shot and killed Detective Tyler Franks with a high-powered rifle. The bullet penetrated his vest. He fired off another shot, which hit the deputy behind Tyler. He was wounded, but thankfully survived. He did suffer major damage to his hand and lost a finger.

The officers at the scene included Tony and other LEACH members. They pulled both officers out of the line of fire, putting themselves in danger. They immediately began CPR on Tyler and first aid for the injured deputy.

After firing those two shots, the boyfriend walked out of his front door with his hands held above his head. He's currently serving a life sentence in prison.

BSO Deputy Franks was only thirty-three, an undercover narcotics cop and an all-around great guy. The narcotics office was on the same floor as LEACH. When I saw him, we always greeted each other, saying things like, "Hey, you guys staying busy?" or "How's it going?" He was a handsome guy who always wore a smile. He seemed to fit in well with his coworkers, who would undoubtedly feel the void created by his loss.

Tyler left behind family and friends who loved him, and a whole team of cops.

This hit too close to home; it happened to two courageous men I had known and worked with. I was devastated by my team's loss and by the loss for this community. Thank goodness Gary had been standing next to me when I learned this sad news.

Tony, Gary, and I attended a large funeral, along with about four thousand of Tyler's colleagues, friends, and family at the Broward

Center for the Performing Arts. We paid our final respects to an American hero who gave his life for his country and to protect children from becoming victimized by that monster.

I held onto Gary's hand tightly during the long, sad service. His support and love supplied me with the needed strength to hold up my heavy heart.

All the LEACH task force members sat together. We cried and hugged each other while the Fraternal Order of Police Drum Corp played "Amazing Grace."

Rest in peace, Tyler.

CHAPTER SIX

THE HUNT FOR THE MISSING CHILDREN

"A two-year-old's gone missing from West Palm Beach," I heard on the other end of the phone.

I had hoped this would be a quiet day so I could catch up on my report-writing. Unfortunately, these types of events don't consider my plans, or anyone else's for that matter.

The duty officer continued. "The grandmother reported the child missing. Even though she doesn't have legal custody of the child, she's been his caretaker since birth. The mother felt her mom was in a better position to take care of her son."

I was writing notes as fast as I could. "Where's the father?"

"He and the mom are estranged, and they claim he has never provided any child support. Anyway, the local police requested FDLE assistance."

"Okay. Where's does the grandmother live? I'll get over there ASAP."

Time was of the essence with these cases, so I left my office to head to the child's maternal grandmother's house without delay. I entered close to the downtown area of West Palm Beach and drove down a tree-lined street. I located the grandmother's address and pulled in front of a well-kept yellow bungalow with a red door.

A stout woman in her sixties with graying black hair answered the door. She wore tropical print clothes in shades of yellow and bright green. Her dark-brown eyes held pools of tears. She introduced herself as the grandmother and the caller, her white teeth contrasting with her dark skin.

She held her hand out to point to the woman standing next to her. She was a smaller version of the grandmother but wearing more demure clothing. "This here's Rosy, my daughter and the baby's mother."

The grandmother cried again while wringing her hands. "I stepped out to go to the grocery store and left 'Little Man' with my daughter. She says the baby's daddy showed up, and a fight started. He grabbed my grandson and left."

"Little Man?" I asked.

"Uh-hum," she said, her voice hoarse with emotion. "That's what we call him."

I made note of this nickname. "Do you know where the father lives?"

Both women shook their heads.

I went into hyper-focus mode, mentally making a list of questions to ask so I would have sufficient information for developing leads. I began by gathering information about the father, including his full name and date of birth.

I went back to my office and asked my analyst to try to locate where the father lived and worked. The computerized public records information revealed a nonviolent criminal history, which admittedly provided some relief. Records gave his last-known residence and business, both of which were in Liberty City near downtown Miami. Knowing I had addresses to start the hunt was always a good thing.

Although there was a chance he may not live there anymore, we had a trail to follow. I also got his picture from his driver's license.

I needed to take a trip down to Liberty City. It was a tough neighborhood, full of thugs and gangbangers. They had no use for the police. Not everyone who lived there was a criminal, though. A lot of good, law-abiding citizens resided in that area due to economics, but they had to endure living in the same neighborhood with the bad guys.

I called my former mentor and partner Mark Harper, an FDLE Special Agent in the MROC (Miami Regional Operations Center).

"Hey, Mark. Mind meeting me in Liberty City? I've got a missing-child case, and the father is a person of interest. He supposedly lives there, and I need to pay him a visit."

"Sure, Floy," Mark said, "I'd be more than happy to."

Mark was always there when I needed him, no matter the time or place. Within an hour, I exited I-95 and headed to NW 79th Street in Miami to meet Mark in the parking lot of the Miami Police stationhouse.

We began our search. We went to the address given, but the father wasn't there. We asked neighbors, who recalled seeing him months ago. They thought he had moved out.

We drove by his worksite, a car repair shop, but we never saw him. We didn't want to approach his boss or any coworkers. We figured they would probably tell him the cops were looking for him, which could cause him to lay low. Instead, we scoured the neighborhood for several blocks near where he lived and worked.

About the time I decided to call it a night, I spotted a bondsman I recognized. He was standing on the street near the father's worksite, looking around. I knew the FDLE had already approved him for its informant list.

I pulled over. Mark stopped his car behind mine.

I exited my vehicle with my case file. I pulled my jacket to the side to reveal my badge. "What's up?" I asked.

He focused on me. "Just searching for a client who skipped a court date."

"I need you to look at a picture."

I showed him the father's picture. I then gave him the address of the father's workplace.

"If you can find the father and Little Man, I'll give you some funds from FDLE." I handed him my business card.

He glanced down at it to read its content. "Special Agent Floy Turner… I surely will let you know if I find them."

Mark and I met up at a small diner outside of Liberty City, where I thanked him and drove home, just in time for dinner with Gary.

Before I could crawl into bed for the night, the bondsman called. He had located the father, and he had Little Man with him.

The good news kept coming. The father agreed to meet me in the morning.

So much for sleep. I was so pleased at how this case was unfolding. I thanked God I had run into that bondsman and that he had come through with this valuable information. I wished all cases with missing children came together like this and that not only were they this easy to solve, but they would turn out so well.

I told the bondsman to have the father and Little Man in court by nine in the morning. Then I called the grandmother and told her and her daughter to be at family court in the morning as well. I would request an emergency custody hearing to clear up this matter.

The following day, everyone showed up at the courtroom on time. The judge requested that the mother, grandmother, father, Little Man, and I go into his chambers for a meeting.

When he asked this adorable two-year-old his name, he answered, "Little Man."

I had to suppress a laugh. I didn't think this child had a clue as to his real name.

All worked out. The whole family agreed for the grandmother to be awarded custody.

I paid the bondsman a couple of hundred dollars out of the FDLE investigative funds. It was a win-win for all.

"Go Back to Chasing Fugitives"

An odd thing happened a week later. FDLE Special Agent Eric Pollen called me.

Eric and I had attended the FDLE Academy together, and we experienced a conflict on the first homicide case I had worked as a special agent. I had tried to stay clear of him ever since.

He was now assigned to the Marshal's Fugitive Task Force. He sounded extremely hostile over the phone. "Floy, what the hell were you thinking using my informant to hunt for a fugitive in Liberty City without notifying me?"

I jumped right back at him. "Eric, are you so desperate for a case that you want to take mine? You do realize that Little Man was a missing two-year-old child who was abducted? You do realize he wasn't a fugitive running from the police? Your informant helped me get that baby back. Go back to chasing fugitives, Eric."

I laughed and hung up on him before he could reply. I wondered if he knew he had gotten all bent out of shape over a missing child. I also wondered if he thought he owned the rights to Liberty City.

Regardless, Eric hadn't changed.

A Mother's Desperation

A month later, I asked Mark to meet me again, this time in Little Havana. I had obtained information on the whereabouts of a mother who had abducted her three children from their custodial father a year ago. She had lost custody due to a drug problem. She and the children allegedly now lived in an apartment in the heart of the Cuban community.

Mark agreed to meet me on Calle Ocho (a.k.a. Eighth Street) at seven in the evening. The clear night allowed the full Miami moon to light up the late-winter sky.

We pulled up to the address given, a three-story gold stucco apartment building with a barrel-tile roof. All the windows appeared to be open with their curtains blowing in the tropical breeze.

Mark and I walked up to the vestibule. I detected the wavering scent of cooking frijoles negros (black beans), platanos maduros (fried bananas), and ropa vieja (pork), all of my favorite foods. The smell of Cuban food enticed my hungry belly, causing me to momentarily wander away from the task at hand.

After stepping inside, I noticed a gangly boy sitting on a step. He was hunched over with his chin in his hands. At first, all I could see was the top of his head covered with curly black hair.

"Hello," I greeted him.

The boy raised his head, giving me a better look at him. He appeared to be about ten years old, and his large, brown eyes held no expression. He wore a blue T-shirt and tan shorts but no shoes.

I identified him as one of the missing children. This recognition quickly drew me back into work mode.

I asked, "Are you Jose?"

He said, "Yes."

"Is your last name Castellanos?"

He gave a big smile. "Yes. I am Jose Castellanos."

I breathed a sigh of relief. The other two children had to be nearby.

"Where are your sisters and mother?"

"I'll take you to our apartment. It's on the third floor."

Mark and I followed Jose upstairs. When we got to the third floor, I noticed how all the apartment doors were opened wide to the oversize hallway. I initially thought this floor looked more like a commune than an apartment building.

Here we were, taking three children from their mother in a commune-type atmosphere. What if a neighbor ran out of his or her apartment to help the mom?

I started to get worried. If this didn't go smoothly, Mark and I would have to fight our way out of it. I used my portable radio to ask the FDLE dispatcher to notify the Miami Police Department of our location and request a patrol unit for assistance.

We followed Jose into a bare-bones apartment with one large room. A simple kitchenette sat off to the side with a three-burner stove and a small under-the-counter refrigerator. Multiple holes could be seen in the green and well-worn linoleum floor. The dirty beige walls contained child-level smudges from dirty fingers.

On the other side of the room, a young woman sat on a full-size bed feeding the smallest child, who looked to be about sixteen months old. The woman looked frail and plain, completely devoid of any makeup. The dark color of her hair presented a striking contrast against her pale complexion. She wore a simple print dress and sandals.

Upon seeing us, her light-green eyes opened wide, and so did her mouth. Her body tensed.

The other little girl, who appeared to be about four years old, ran behind the woman and peeked around her legs. Her wide eyes pushed her eyebrows up so high that they almost hid under the fine wisps of dark hair falling from her hairline.

The woman matched the picture we had been given. I had no doubt it was the mother.

I said, "Mrs. Castellanos, we're here because you've violated your child-custody agreement. We need to take the children with us tonight. Tomorrow morning, you need to be at the Broward Courthouse by nine for an emergency custody hearing."

As an afterthought, I said, "Please walk with us. You can help us get the children in my car to help them feel secure."

I wanted to make this incident go as smoothly as possible. If she became excited, Mark and I could end up in a free-for-all, battling her neighbors. I also knew these children would be upset when we took them away from their mother. I didn't want them to endure more unnecessary trauma.

Mrs. Castellanos nodded. I believed that deep down, she was a good mother who tried to care for her children. I don't think she understood the system. I'm not sure I understood the system either, nor did I like it.

We walked out with the children and their mother to my vehicle. Several of her neighbors stood in their doorways and watched us with interest as we passed. Thankfully, no one tried to interfere.

As we exited the building, a MPD unit drove up and stopped. I guess that was our backup. I waved to acknowledge their presence as I walked to my trunk to retrieve the car seats we always kept with us.

Mrs. Castellanos helped me place the children in the seats and kissed them goodbye. When she faced me, tears had pooled in her eyes.

Jose walked over to me. He whispered, "I'm glad you came for me. I've been wanting to go to school, but my mother wouldn't let me. She was afraid the authorities would find out she didn't have custody."

My heart sank. "When was the last time you went to school, Jose?"

"Not for over six months."

I forced myself to smile to encourage him. "Well, six months isn't too long. You'll get caught up before you know it."

He looked down and nodded.

Victims of family abductions usually don't attend school and are denied any meaningful education, not to mention proper medical or dental care. Their names are changed. They're taught to lie to people about their circumstances. They begin to fear authority. They might be told the other parent died. In my opinion, the children suffer emotional consequences from these circumstances.

Jose was the anomaly. He struck me as a kid who was desperate to go to school. Unfortunately, he had been neglected through this situation.

I hated taking children away from their mothers. However, my personal feelings didn't matter; I was mandated to uphold the law.

<u>Kidnapper with a Violent Past</u>

There were times, however, that I found removing children from parents a gratifying task. In another case that year, nothing made me happier than the idea of taking little Henry away from his dad.

A few months after the Castellanos case, I received a call from Maryland State Police Detective Susan Hightower. "Special Agent Turner, I've been tracking the cellphone of a Jamaican fugitive wanted for attempted murder. He abducted his three-year-old son from Baltimore six months ago. Unfortunately, every time we find him, he manages to disappear again.

"The most recent hit we've gotten on his cell phone was a tower in West Palm Beach. An agent from the U.S. Marshal's Office helped me narrow down the location within a few blocks."

She paused before continuing. "I need help firming up the exact location. I also need help getting a warrant. Most importantly, I need help rescuing this child."

I told Susan I would help her with all three of her needs.

She said, "I have to inform you that this guy favors machetes as his weapon of choice. In fact, he sliced his former wife with one, and as a result, he's wanted on a felony warrant for attempted murder."

A shiver went down my spine, but that was good information to know. I then headed up to West Palm Beach to search Susan's established area, calling Gary since he worked in the Palm Beach field office.

He agreed to help me out. I met him at his office, and we both drove through the designated area, targeting the spots where the cell tower had shown the dad using his cellphone.

Susan called again while Gary and I drove around. "Floy, I've been able to coordinate the cellphone tower triangulation through the U.S. Marshal's Office Fugitive Task Force. We now have an address."

We located the address right away. The faded-yellow apartment complex consisted of two connected apartments in the front and a stand-alone apartment in the rear near an alleyway. Dying grass, overgrown trees, and broken concrete sidewalks made up the curb appeal, or lack thereof.

Because the father was a violent fugitive, we needed more manpower in case he confronted us with a weapon. To that end, we knocked on the neighbors' doors to gather information. They confirmed that the fugitive lived in the apartment, but no one admitted to ever seeing a child with him.

I called Susan and gave her our findings. I went back to my office, but Gary stayed behind to observe the small stand-alone building. He also talked with the Palm Beach County Sheriff's Office to coordinate its SWAT team's entrance into the apartment building.

I quickly drafted a search warrant and took it to the duty judge, who signed it. I then met the deputy marshal who had tracked the cellphone and the SWAT commander and his team at a shopping strip three blocks from the father's apartment. I showed him the signed warrant and briefed him on all the details we had learned about the father's criminal history, his felony warrant, his weapon of choice, and the possibility that the child might be in the apartment.

The commander was diligent in verifying the information and evaluating the situation. I drove him to the area so he could assess the layout of the apartment. He then gathered his SWAT members and briefed them.

He, his team, and the deputy marshal followed Gary and me back to the apartment. Everyone took their positions upon arrival.

SWAT strategically approached the apartment door. They used a battering ram to breach the door and then threw in flashbang grenades to create a distraction. Two SWAT members entered first, their weapons held at eye level and led the way. I entered next followed by the deputy marshal.

The father's eyes opened wide when he saw these warriors coming through his front doorway. Another set of SWAT members grabbed him and forced him to the floor to handcuff him.

I laid the search warrant in front of his face. The deputy marshal took custody of the fugitive father.

A screaming little boy was hiding behind the kitchen counter. I could only imagine how terrifying this scene was to a three-year-old. A SWAT member picked the child up and carried him outside. I went ahead of him to meet the victim advocate and DCF investigator who I had standing by. Henry went to DCF for the night.

I called Susan with the news, my voice light and excited. "We have Henry's father in custody, and Henry's at DCF. Can his mom get a flight to make the emergency hearing in the Palm Beach County Courthouse by midmorning tomorrow?"

"Fantastic!" Susan said. "I'll make the arrangements for a Maryland State Police aircraft to fly Henry's mom to Florida early in the morning. Her name's Judy Morgan. The pilot's going to need to return immediately after dropping the mother off, so he won't be able to bring them back."

"That's okay," I said. "I'll call the National Center for Missing and Exploited Children. I'll ask them to buy the tickets to fly Henry and his mother home tomorrow evening."

"Thank you, Floy... for everything."

Susan and I discussed the arrangements for me to pick up Judy in the morning. I would then take her to the hearing.

Our plan worked. I picked Judy up at Signature Aviation Terminal, a small airport that catered to private planes.

When I saw Henry's mom, I couldn't grasp how someone like her had become involved with this fugitive. She was quite attractive, with skin the color of creamy chocolate, light-brown eyes, and a slim build. She piled her long dark hair into a round bun high up on the back of her neck.

She wore a nice pair of black slacks and turquoise blouse complemented by a paisley print scarf wrapped around her neck. She came across as well-educated, working as a professional in the healthcare field.

I took Judy to the DCF halfway house to see Henry before the hearing. On the way, I put my investigator hat on because I had just one burning question to ask. "How did you meet Henry's father?"

She said, "My friend introduced him to me. She was his cousin. I was never told about his past or that he had been married and attacked his wife. I fell for him. Once I became pregnant, he became controlling. We never married. I left him and was awarded complete custody of Henry."

I kept on my best poker face, but in my mind, I wanted to know more. Judy studied my face for a moment before continuing.

"In a weak moment, I permitted him to visit Henry. I knew in my gut I was taking a chance, but he promised me he just wanted to see his son for a short visit. I didn't know he was wanted by the law."

I have heard many stories like Judy's with other crime victims. They're manipulated and feel sorry for the offender. She paid a big price for not following her instincts.

Judy had packed a suitcase for Henry, including fresh clothes, bath items, a comb, a brush, and his favorite snacks.

I signed us in at the halfway house. When she saw him, she broke down in tears. She fell to her knees and held out her arms as he ran into them without hesitation. She hugged him tight and kissed the top of his little head. "My darling little boy is filthy. I need to wash him."

Fortunately, DCF had a bathtub in this facility.

After Henry's bath, Judy said, "This is not the happy, well-adjusted child I had six months ago. Henry's personality has drastically changed."

I took Henry and Judy to the hearing. The judge released Henry from DCF back to his mother's custody. Then Henry, Judy, and I ate lunch before driving to the Miami International Airport. We drove for the next two hours in afternoon traffic.

First, we stopped at the Miami-Dade Airport Police Substation. The sergeant assigned to the Airport District shuttled us to the American Airlines counter. The National Center for Missing and Exploited Children (NCMEC) had purchased the tickets and had them waiting for us.

The sergeant brought along a stuffed blue dolphin. Henry clasped his new stuffed animal in his arms.

By the time Henry entered the TSA checkpoint, he became wild when the TSA agent took his dolphin and placed it in the screening bin. Henry screamed, cried, and thrashed in his mother's arms. She kept a firm hold on him and kept reassuring him that he and the toy were going to be okay.

The Miami-Dade sergeant informed the TSA agents that this child was a kidnapping victim. One of the TSA agents gave the dolphin back to Henry, but he didn't want it. He continued throwing a fit.

Seeing his meltdown as a result of the dramatic rescue, being held captive by his father, and having his mother removed from his care was heartbreaking. These were complex situations for a child to deal with, and I felt helpless.

We ushered this uncontrollable bundle onto the plane. I could see the passengers all looking horrified as Henry continued his tantrum. By the time I disembarked the plane, Henry's screams had become whimpers.

I maintained contact with Judy for quite a while afterward. I learned that she put Henry in therapy for a couple of years. I also stayed in touch with Susan for over a year. She followed Henry's slow progress of returning to the sweet and happy little boy he had been before his abduction.

A few years later, Susan and I unexpectedly met face-to-face. She showed up as a participant in one of my law enforcement training classes in California.

We were so glad to finally get to meet each other.

<u>State Law Enforcement Officer of the Year</u>

In 2004, I located fifteen missing children, all of whom were returned to their families. As a result, I received the honor of being chosen for the State Law Enforcement Officer of the Year Award at Florida's annual Missing Children's Day. This governor always presented this prestigious award to the state law enforcement officer who had made a substantial impact for locating missing children.

Both of my daughters flew to Tallahassee for this event, along with my favorite cousin Bruce and his wife Linda. Gary couldn't attend. He had just passed the test to be promoted to Special Agent Supervisor and was expected to attend a Homeland Security Training in New York at that same time.

I wished he could have made it, but I understood. When both spouses in a marriage are in law enforcement, coordinating events such as this presents a challenge.

As I stood on the podium with Governor Bush and John Walsh of *America's Most Wanted*, I felt humbled and moved to receive such a prestigious award. Of course, my primary thoughts were on all the children who still needed to be rescued and those who sadly would never be home again.

When Gary returned from New York, I was surprised and thrilled when he gave me my first-ever necklace-and-bracelet set from Tiffany's as a remembrance of this important event.

CHAPTER SEVEN

DOMESTIC MINOR SEX TRAFFICKING

I navigated the heavy traffic and a few minor fender-benders along I-95 to Miami.

Glad to be out of my office, I took in the beautiful spring day that made the drive more bearable. The sky seemed to create its own unique color palette, finger painting a beautiful combination of pink and blue as its background. The sun tried its best to peek out of the white billowing clouds.

The breeze caused the palm trees along the highway to sway as if they were dancing to a slow and rhythmic melody. Still, the day would heat up as it always did this time of year, making me thankful to have finished my daily run first thing this morning.

My mind travelled back to today's mission. Judge Naomi Silverman had summoned me to her courtroom in Miami's Juvenile Justice Center (JJC). Since I didn't have any active cases in her court, I could only surmise she wanted to speak to me about a specific child or situation.

I had never met Judge Silverman, but I had a tremendous amount of respect for her. She had earned a reputation as a no-nonsense judge and as a staunch advocate for children. Consequently, my supervisor encouraged me to see where and how I could assist the court. He knew she was constantly looking for new methods and tactics for the judicial system to attain perfect justice.

I, on the other hand, had acquired a similar reputation. With my many appearances in family court, the court administrators knew me and/or they knew my name. I think they saw me as someone who combed the streets to locate missing children. They weren't far off the mark.

At the same time, the Department of Children and Families (DCF) assigned some of its investigators to search for children and locate them for family court. In reality, their caseload didn't allow them the time to work long investigations. Plus, the low pay acted as a culprit that created constant employee turnover.

Finally, I made it to the outskirts of Miami. My watch showed ten-fifteen.

I drove west across State Road 836. Fortunately, at that hour, most of the heavy traffic traveled eastbound into the city.

After exiting at NW 27th Avenue, I headed north a few blocks, passing by an area with several Cuban butcher shops. Heavy chains held pigs suspended in midair as they waited for burial in some backyard barbeque pit.

The Juvenile Justice Center was on the fringe of Liberty City. Like all of Miami's courthouses, it provided limited space for parking. Many of the marked police cars haphazardly parked over the slowly dissipating patches of grass that receded under the weight and traction of heavy tires.

I jumped a curb and found a small area between two palm trees for my unmarked beige Chevy Blazer. Its dark-tinted windows were a common trademark of South Florida police cars.

I threw my blue light on the dashboard and briskly walked to this ill-kept concrete building. One word to describe this poorly designed government structure was "monstrosity."

Cigarette butts, candy wrappers, discarded chewing gum, and crumpled napkins containing half-eaten hotdogs littered the dirty courtyard. I tackled my climb up the stairs, dodging the folks sitting on the steps. Their only apparent reason for being there was to wait for their respective assigned judge.

Most of the court cases had been cleared by the time I arrived. Judge Silverman sat inside her courtroom, finishing her remaining docket.

She looked attractive and ageless, considering she had been on the bench for the past twenty-five-plus years. She kept a feminine air to her role of immense authority, accessorizing the customary black robe with a small strand of pearls. Matching pearl earrings sat on each side of her narrow face.

She maintained a professional appearance, parting her black hair down the middle and pulling it severely back into a clip at the base of her neck. Her black-framed glasses sat on top of her head, like a tiara.

I sat down on one of the hard, oak benches in the very back of the room and waited. Once she disposed of the remaining cases, she smiled and motioned me forward to her bench.

"Special Agent Turner, I would like you to follow me to my chambers," she said.

We both exited the courtroom through a side door.

Judge Silverman's office was very cheerful in comparison to the courtroom. Framed pictures drawn by children covered her tan walls. A dark wooden desk sat on top of rich, red carpet.

She held her hand toward an upholstered plaid chair. "Please have a seat, Agent Turner."

After sitting in the black leather chair behind her heavy desk, she smiled again. "I guess you're wondering why I asked you to come here."

I returned her smile. "Yes, ma'am."

"Someone in Tallahassee told me how great you are at locating missing children."

I smiled, admittedly proud and honored that my colleagues and the higher echelon perceived me in that way and that this judge reached out for my help as a result.

Without waiting for a reply, she told me the story of Celestine Miot, a fifteen-year-old Haitian-American girl. Celestine was a victim and witness in an FBI sex-trafficking case. She had been before Judge Silverman for truancy a number of times, and the judge saw potential in her because she was very bright. However, the lack of support or initiative from her family prevented consistency in her school attendance.

The smile left Judge Silverman's face. "Celestine has run away from the group home where she was living. I thought a pimp might have sent one of his other girls to convince Celestine to leave, either through manipulation or threats."

I nodded. I knew how pimps involved in minor sex trafficking used this common tactic to pull a girl into, or back into prostitution and into his stable.

Judge Silverman placed clasped hands on her desk. "I believe this child could be salvaged with intense therapy. I need you to locate her and bring her back to juvenile court where I can personally monitor her progress."

She scanned my face. "But that's not all. There's a pending case against Celestine's trafficker. Since she has agreed to testify against him, I'm worried that this trafficker is the one who has her."

Two thoughts raced through my mind simultaneously. One, this child might be in danger, and her pimp could have kidnapped her. I concurred with the judge that Celestine might have been lured back into a trap by another girl who might have been part of the pimp's stable.

There were many dependent children who had no family members looking after them. They became targets and easy prey for sex traffickers because they suffered from low self-esteem, and/or these victims often ran away from shelters to return to their trafficker multiple times.

These ruthless pimps used psychological techniques as a means to obtain power over these children. The pimps became their lovers and protectors. They gave them love and gifts coupled with severe physical force and often drugs to maintain control and destroy any will to resist.

I didn't ask Judge Silverman why she called me instead of the FBI. Maybe she felt more comfortable having a state agent assigned to assist and decided to reach out to the governor's office for FDLE assistance.

But Celestine was a witness in a federal FBI case. For all I knew, they may have been looking for her. Regardless, I knew this child needed to be placed in a secure setting that she couldn't walk away from or leave. She could then receive long-term psychological treatment, hopefully with understanding and loving support from caregivers. Back then, unfortunately, finding a facility for human trafficking victims was difficult.

I immediately hit the streets. By that time, my stomach reminded me that I had missed lunch. I drove to La Carreta and dosed myself with my favorite comfort food: a Cuban lunch.

I took my time eating. I needed to speak with the Miami Police Department's Vice Unit, and they didn't start their shift until six that evening. At this point, there was no reason to drive back to my office in Fort Lauderdale or my home in Palm Beach.

To pass the time, I took care of some paperwork in my car. I knew a late-night escapade awaited me, so I called Gary and told him not to expect me home for dinner.

Karen Kool worked in the Miami FBI office, so I called her to see if she wanted to meet for a light dinner.

She said, "Wish I could, but I have late-night surveillance. What are you doing in Miami tonight?"

"Looking for a juvenile witness who has been a victim of human trafficking. She's supposed to testify in federal court on an FBI case, but a state judge knows this victim from state court and requested through FDLE that I locate her."

"Oh, I wish I could help you out now, but I can get on it tomorrow morning. I'll look into which FBI agent has the case and connect you two."

Admittedly, I was disappointed we wouldn't be working together that night. Karen and I worked well together. I simply said, "Thanks, Karen. I'll touch base with you tomorrow if I still need help."

I looked at my watch. Vice's shift would be starting soon, so I drove to where the MPD Vice Unit turned out. When I arrived, I recognized some of the detectives. We had worked together on the case of a serial killer who had killed several prostitutes.

Inside, the squad was just finishing up their briefing. I located Sergeant Ramos and told him about Celestine and the judge's interest in this case.

I asked, "Would you and your squad help me locate her?"

He smiled. "Absolutely, Floy. I'll make sure you have plenty of assistance."

I provided Sergeant Ramos and the squad with the address of the group home and the name, pedigree, and description of the pimp out on bond and awaiting trial.

The vice cops agreed that if Celestine was still in Miami, she would be working "the track," an area known for prostitution, located along Biscayne Boulevard. This road runs parallel to the beautiful Intercoastal Waterway, but that's where the beauty ends. The pavement snakes its way through blighted, decaying buildings where rooms are rented by the hour.

Sergeant Ramos said, "I'll have my team work that area tonight."

I was grateful for his help. We planned to cover about eighty city blocks. My gut feeling told me that I would probably find Celestine in the northern section on the outer edge of the neighborhood known as Little Haiti.

Three two-person teams helped me scour this area. One of the teams located Celestine on the track, walking down U.S. 1 around NW 81 Street around two-thirty in the morning. They brought her into their department's vice unit.

I entered the interview room with one of the vice detectives, a handsome Hispanic man who wore his long brown hair in a ponytail. I sat down at the metallic table across from Celestine while the detective stood nearby. I studied her for a moment before speaking.

"Celestine, I'm taking you into custody overnight. In the morning, I'll take you before Judge Silverman." I then proceeded to cuff her.

She glared at me and pouted. Then she mouthed off. "You are a wicked, white bitch. You got no reason to be jacking me up in my hood."

Evidently, I had pissed off Celestine. Not only had I just taken away her freedom, but I deprived her of making money for her "daddy." Many pimps used the name *daddy* to cultivate and grow their "family unit" to further their method of control.

Celestine's bond with her pimp blinded her to the reality of the situation. She didn't appreciate my authority or my rescuing her. In her mind, she didn't need rescuing. Children of human trafficking often don't see themselves as victims.

I didn't expect anything different from her. I've worked enough with these teenage victims to know what to anticipate. Many come from dysfunctional families and don't understand that love and respect are intertwined.

I booked this victim into the Juvenile Detention Center. I then arranged for her to be in front of Judge Silverman the next morning. I recognized the inappropriateness of the Juvenile Detention Center for Celestine. She wasn't a criminal, but a victim.

Unfortunately, it turned out to be the only place I could keep her secure for the night. Judge Silverman could then have a heart-to-heart talk with her in the morning and place her in Save Our

Children, a program offered by a nonprofit organization to rehabilitate victims of human trafficking. It offered psychological services, intense therapy sessions, educational opportunities, and mentoring in a secure environment.

Before I left the detention center, I briefly searched Celestine's face. I gave her a small smile and looked directly and softly into her eyes. "The only friend you have who can help you is Judge Silverman. She cares about you. I hope you can live up to what she thinks you are capable of becoming."

Her pout turned into a scowl of hatred. She narrowed her eyes and jutted her chin forward to get in the last word, or in this case, words. "Fuck you, horny, scrawny bitch."

She was an example of why many law enforcement officers become jaded. This type of beyond-unappreciative attitude made them not want to do much to help street kids, and many chose to leave them where they found them—on the street. They didn't want to commit to the four to eight hours needed to process them through the Juvenile Assessment Center. The police or some judicial circuits categorized some of these kids as juvenile delinquents instead of recognizing them as victims of sex trafficking.

I believed what I told Celestine. I believed that if anyone would save her, it would be Naomi Silverman. This woman was on her side and a person I will always admire as a voice for children.

I woke up the next morning at around nine o'clock, feeling the sleep deprivation from only a short four hours of shut-eye. I didn't possess the energy to go out for my morning run.

After two cups of strong coffee, I found enough energy to call Karen. "Tell your FBI buddies I located their star witness. If they want to know where she is, they can call me."

When Celestine was brought before the judge, she had noticeably calmed down. I had hoped it was because she had taken my words to heart about Judge Silverman.

Although she refused to look at me, her attitude had nonetheless done a one-eighty. She seemed ashamed and afraid. She promised the judge that she would do her best in the program.

For the next six months, Judge Silverman worked with Celestine and mentored her as she progressed in the Save Our Children program. This was plenty of time for her to have a positive influence on Celestine and undo a lot of the brainwashing her pimp subjected her to.

 It worked. Celestine testified against the trafficker in court. He was sentenced to ten years in a federal prison.

Judge Silverman called me a few years later to let me know that Celestine had finished high school and was headed to college. Celestine is one of the few who got out of *the life*.

From School Girl to Trafficked Victim

The cool and overcast mid-January day may have been ideal weather to sip cocoa by a fireplace and read a book, but I didn't have that luxury. Instead, I needed to sit in my office to catch up on writing reports and reviewing case files. Television and movies don't depict this part of law enforcement.

The tedious and methodical need to capture all investigative activities in detailed documentation is paramount for further investigations and prosecution. An adage can be heard in law enforcement circles that if it's not written and documented, then it didn't happen.

I had just gotten back an hour earlier from the Miami-Dade County/Monroe County Child Death Review Board meeting. I attended this meeting every month as part of my responsibilities as the FDLE Regional Crimes Against Children Coordinator. I also attended the Broward County Child Death Review Board meetings as time allowed.

These boards provided a multi-disciplined community-based approach to review facts related to child abuse deaths and contributing factors. The goal was to improve agency response through compiling detailed data.

I leaned back in my chair, breathing deeply, trying to relieve the stress from my morning meeting.

My supervisor appeared in the doorway of my office. "Tallahassee wants you to find a missing child who's a victim of sex trafficking."

I leaned forward to focus on him. "What are the details?"

He started reading from the one of the sheets of paper in his hand. "The victim's name is Cynthia Glasson. She's a fifteen-year-old from Putnam County, New York. She is believed to be in the Miami area because she called her mother from the Miami jail. She also told her mom that she had left New York with someone named Snowflake. Her mother sent the Florida governor an email requesting state assistance, which is why I'm standing in your doorway right now." He handed me the file.

I recognized the gravity of the situation. I needed to locate Cynthia, recover her, and keep Governor Bush's office notified of my progress.

I read through the request from the governor. Attached was the email that Cynthia's mom had sent to Governor Bush. Prior to my involvement, Cynthia lived at home. She hung with a bad crowd, smoked pot, and experimented with other recreational drugs.

Her father was a police officer in New York City. His knee-jerk reaction to Cynthia's bad behavior caused him to ship her off to a boarding school in Pennsylvania. After Christmas vacation, Cynthia's father dropped her off at the Port Authority in New York City so she could take a bus back to her school, but she never arrived.

I called her father. The NYPD had opened a case, and the dad had conducted his own investigation at the Port Authority. The father had the Port Authority Police pull the video. They showed Cynthia sitting at the bus terminal when a pimp's bottom girl approached her.

Vice verified that Snowflake was a "bottom girl" who had prior arrests for prostitution and solicitation in New York. Despite the name, the *bottom* happens to be the highest in hierarchy in the pimp world. They act as recruiters and can be found anywhere young girls were, such as middle schools, high schools, malls, online, and other favorite venues for youngsters.

I had only heard the street name Snowflake used by white women, which clued me in that the bottom girl was a white female.

From my past encounters with domestic sex trafficking, I knew the recruiting tactics involved. Pimps and bottom-girl recruiters promised glamour, beautiful clothes, jewelry, excitement, and money to their perspective victims.

I figured that if Snowflake had lured Cynthia to Miami, it was with the same kind of promises. After all, most fifteen-year-old girls have seen television shows and movies depicting the fun-in-the-sun life of Miami.

Bringing Cynthia to another state was a common trend incorporated into the pimps' operations. It involved moving "fresh meat" far away from their home locations to work in the sex trade and giving them new names and dates of birth in case they were encountered by the cops. These pimps frequently moved them to such "tracks" on the east coast, such as Queens, Atlantic City, Atlanta, Orlando, and Miami Beach.

"Tracks" were the locations where "working girls" prostituted themselves, walking the streets to look for johns. These areas usually consisted of sidewalks near strip clubs, bars, hotels, or in the seedy parts of town where they became known to the johns, taxi drivers, truck drivers, and hotel workers.

Prior to her stint in the Miami jail, a Miami Beach Police Officer spotted Cynthia and questioned her. Her inexperience in this world caused her to give her correct date of birth. She then realized she hadn't followed her pimp's directions, so she told the officer she made a mistake. She then gave him a date of birth that made her eighteen.

The officer crossed out the fifteen-year-old date of birth on the arrest affidavit and wrote the fake one over it. This displayed a clear I-don't-give-a-crap attitude. I always wondered how this officer would have felt if this were his daughter.

Cynthia was taken to the Miami-Dade County Jail and booked as an adult at eight in the evening. She was allowed one telephone call at nine-thirty. That's when she called home and told her mother where she was.

Cynthia cried into the phone. "I'm in jail in Miami. I'm afraid, and I want to come home." She then told her mother about meeting Snowflake and how she had been tricked into coming to Miami Beach. She also told her mother that someone named Mello made her do bad things, and she got arrested because of it.

As soon as she hung up, Mrs. Glasson hurriedly dialed the jail and asked for the shift commander. "Hello. I'm Cynthia Glasson's mother. She's in your jail, and she's a juvenile. The Putnam County Sheriff's Office is faxing you a copy of the pickup order."

The evening shift ended at eleven that night. Despite Mrs. Glasson's information and discussions with the earlier shift commander, none of her efforts mattered. No one notified the midnight shift commander about her juvenile daughter being locked up in the adult section of the jail.

Cynthia was bonded out of the Miami-Dade County Jail at midnight by Bondsman Leroy Brown. He had earned the reputation in Miami of being the go-to bondsman for all the pimps. He drove Cynthia to the hotel where Mello retook possession of his property.

Unfortunately, I didn't find out what had transpired until forty-eight hours later. Fortunately, the little bit of information Cynthia gave to her mother was valuable in getting a trace on Cynthia and the street name of the culprits involved.

Angry at the turn of events, my first order of business was to locate Leroy Brown. I found his address on the state's bail bonds person registration system. I wanted to find out where Mello was and find Cynthia, so I drove to his house on a street lined with single family homes in Opa Locka.

I pulled in front of Leroy's house. I radioed the dispatcher to report my location in case I didn't make it out of Opa Locka. I then called FDLE Special Agent Mark Harper to back me up. I thought I may need another cop with me just in case Leroy didn't take to me in a friendly way.

Mark said, "Sure thing, Floy. I'm just finishing up having dinner out with my family. I'll drop them off at home, pick up my service car and head that way."

For the next two hours, I studied Leroy's residence with the nice, red barrel-tile roof. The small lot that held his white concrete stucco home didn't have enough room for a garage. He surrounded his small yard, including his front yard, with the most common type of Miami fence—a four-foot chain link. A nondescript chain-link gate allowed access to the walkway. Leroy's yard contained two large Doberman Pinschers, one red and one black, each weighing over eighty pounds.

When Leroy finally drove up in his gold Caddy, I got out of my car and met him at the gate.

"Hi, Leroy." I greeted him with a smile, "Special Agent Floy Turner with FDLE. We need to talk."

"Sure," he said, returning my smile. "Let's go inside."

Although he acted nice and friendly toward me, I knew better than to trust this dirtbag. These guys only cared about one thing: getting their bonds covered.

I felt okay with his dogs since they wagged their stumpy tails when they saw us. I followed him inside without any fear of being bitten.

As soon as we entered the cool confines of his cozy abode, I took a seat in an expensive wingback chair in his living room, marveling at his granite fireplace. His traditional-style furnishings seemed out of place for this run-down Florida neighborhood. I thought they would fit better in a colonial home in Virginia.

About the time I sat down in Leroy's fancy living room, Mark called my cell phone. "Floy, I'm outside at the gate. I need these dogs put away so I can come inside."

Once Leroy put his dogs in the back, Mark joined us. I felt more relaxed having him with me. I introduced Leroy to Mark, and then proceeded to explain the facts of life to Leroy. I reminded him that he had a Florida license to operate as a bondman, and I could investigate his involvement of working for a pimp who trafficked underage girls.

I ended my pep talk by telling him, "I'm your new best friend. I promise you, Leroy, I'll show up at your home every day until I find Cynthia."

Leroy's smile dissolved as his eyes darted between Mark and me. Then he starting talking. He told me he worked for Michael Gate, who went by the street name Mello. He had heard from some of Mello's other victims how he operated, giving them drugs and raping them.

"He contacted me to bail out Cynthia," Leroy said.

By the time Mark and I left Leroy's house, we were armed with information. We discovered that we could find Mello, a.k.a. Michael Gate, in Miami Beach at the Castle Hotel.

I had my analyst run a criminal history on our Mr. Gate. I learned he was a convicted felon who served time at Riker's Island jail in New York.

Next, I needed to find out more about Snowflake. I figured I'd start with Miami Beach Police Department's Vice Unit, since Miami Beach was where Cynthia had been arrested. That provided a link to Mello's other girls who worked there.

MBPD's Vice gave me Snowflake's arrest record. She had been arrested for prostitution many times. She would serve time and then be released, as is typical for prostitution cases.

Within her file, I was able to acquire her real name, picture, and pedigree. According to detectives, Snowflake had traveled to New York to recruit young girls like Cynthia and bring them to Miami, but they had never been able to make a case on that. From Miami Beach's intelligence on Mello and his operation, I was also able to link Mello and Snowflake as co-conspirators in previous New York cases.

Mark and I headed to the Castle Hotel to find Mello. When we entered the lobby, I observed an array of countries and cultures represented by British and German tourists, elderly Jewish couples speaking Yiddish, working girls (prostitutes), and pimps.

Mark and I sat in the lobby to surveil it. I spotted a couple of working girls with "Mello" tattooed across their chests above their skimpy tops. Pimps brand their "stable" with their street names. In Miami, some of the pimps took their property to the 79th Street Flea Market for tattooing. I silently prayed that Cynthia had not yet been branded.

At least we knew we were in the right location.

Mark and I followed some of the Mello girls to their rooms. We stopped them as they opened the door.

"Hey, ladies," I said in a louder-than-normal voice. "I'm looking for Cynthia." I looked around at the blank faces. I made an exaggerated sniff in the air. "It would be in your best interest to help me locate her. If you help me out, I won't bust you on marijuana possession." I was taking a gamble, making the assumption that because I smelled pot on them, I would find weed in their rooms laying in plain view.

Still nothing.

"How about Michael Gate? How can I find him?"

This time, I did get a reaction, though it wasn't any more helpful. They murmured, "Michael who?" "Never heard of him?" "Don't know him" and a few more similar responses.

I didn't believe them. "How strange," I said. "You don't know Michael Gate, yet you have his brand in one-inch letters across your chest."

Mark asked, "Mind if we look around?"

Some nodded while others said, "Sure, why not?"

Mark and I entered their rooms and proceeded to search all four of them. I smelled marijuana in every room. One even had a large pit-bulldog that hadn't been house trained. That hotel room stunk.

After our search, we gathered their IDs and ran background checks on them to make sure they were all indeed adults. We then spoke to each girl. Fortunately, we gained some info from a couple who were sympathetic to Cynthia's plight. In exchange for this information, we promised not to "rat them out."

One girl said, "Yeah, I know her. I felt really bad for her. She was just a kid, you know. Mello gave her weed and other drugs." She shook her head. "He took her to some big, fancy hotel in South Beach. That's where he takes all the new girls so he can rape them over and over again. Poor thing."

I cringed.

She continued, and I let her. "He does that for a few days. Mello and Snowflake tell these new girls they'll be working for him. Then they're sent off to the tracks in Miami Beach."

Although this was typical, I felt my stomach churn big time. Cynthia had evidently received a crash course in hooking.

In a very short two weeks, Cynthia had gone from middle-class school girl with good family values and parents who loved her to human trafficking victim. She now belonged to Mello.

Cynthia was gone, and we suspected Mello had moved her. I thought maybe Leroy had snitched us out. This upset me tremendously, especially having made so much progress and getting so close to her trail. Mello was a few steps ahead of us, though.

The next day, Mark and I visited Leroy at his office. It was all I could do to maintain calm. "Where did Mello take Cynthia, Leroy?"

He glanced down before glancing back up. He couldn't look us in our eyes. "Queens, New York."

This news made me even angrier. I had hoped we would locate her in Florida.

I suspected that Mello knew Leroy had given us a lot of information and that we were close on his heels. Moving Cynthia to New York before we could take away his money-making product was probably more profitable.

We began to work with the NYPD Vice Unit. I sent them my investigative notes, and we exchanged phone calls for months. We also kept Cynthia's father in the loop. I suspected he was travelling the whole borough of Queens looking for her.

Cynthia stayed on the street for a few more months. Mello sold her to a second pimp who kept her working between Queens and Atlantic City.

Then, one day, her mother called me. She said Cynthia finally escaped from her pimps. One night when working in Queens, she knew her new pimp was in a diner eating, so she ran. Fortunately, she didn't have far to run since her family home was in Queens.

I let out a big sigh of relief before a smile erupted on my face. That was wonderful news. I was so thankful she had escaped from her captors and prayed she would get the help she needed to recover from this horrific experience.

After working this case for ten months, Cynthia would finally get justice. She gave the NYPD information on Mello and the other pimp who had been working her too. Fortunately, both were already in their database. She identified them through a photo array.

Because these pimps moved frequently on a circuit from Queens, New York to Atlantic City, New Jersey to Atlanta, Georgia, to Orlando and Miami, Florida, locating them took some time.

A year after Cynthia's return home, the NYPD finally arrested both traffickers. They were prosecuted and sentenced to twelve years in prison.

Following the close of the New York case, I wanted to prosecute Mello for trafficking in Florida, but the family didn't think it was in Cynthia's best interest to pursue another prosecution. I relented. I went to the court on Cynthia's prostitution case in Miami Beach and requested the case be dropped. I told them Cynthia was a child victim of sex trafficking. The judge and the prosecutor both agreed.

I called Mrs. Glasson several times during the year after Cynthia came home. I wanted to check on her progress. Recovering from the mental and physical trauma of life on the streets can be very difficult under the best of circumstances.

During my last call, Mrs. Glasson said, "This is a hard transition. We're hoping for the best."

I never called again. This family needed to move on without any interference from me.

I think of Cynthia often and wonder how her life has been. I also question how a child victim recovers from a crime that robbed her of her youth and innocence, not to mention her human dignity and self-worth.

Thank God, He made the human spirit resilient.

CHAPTER EIGHT

CHILD ABDUCTION RESPONSE TEAM

Intertwined with society are two-legged monsters who obsess and prey on the most vulnerable members of our society—our children.

We haven't always had the best tools to address these tragic incidents. Uniform protocols and procedures to ensure an immediate response for missing and abducted children didn't exist, yet every second counted in finding that child. The fact that detectives had to first organize before beginning a search took a huge bite out of precious time.

Over the years, much-needed progress had been made, but these improvements came too late for too many children.

When John Walsh's son Adam was abducted and murdered in 1981, police told the parents that a child must be missing for twenty-four hours before he or she could be entered into the FBI National Crime Information Center (NCIC), the central database for tracking crime in the U.S.

Then in 1996, nine-year-old Amber Hagerman was abducted and murdered in Arlington, Texas. Sadly, no system was in place to find her in time. The AMBER Alert was soon instituted as a crucial tool to assist the police in finding a missing child more quickly by broadcasting information to the media and general public. Although named after little Amber, the alert is also an acronym for "America's Missing: Broadcast Emergency Response."

By 2005, every state, U.S. territory, and Washington D.C. participated in the AMBER Alert program. A partnership formed between law enforcement, broadcasters/media, transportation agencies, emergency management agencies, telecommunications/call centers, other public safety agencies, and child protection organizations.

Fifteen years after Adam's abduction-murder, President George W. Bush signed the Adam Walsh Child Protection and Safety Act into law in 2006. It mandated entering missing children into the NCIC (National Crime Information Center) within two hours of the time of the reported activity.

Carlie Brucia and CART

The abduction of Carlie Brucia on February 1, 2004, moved progress forward even more in the finding of missing children.

On a cool winter evening, while most people were watching the Super Bowl, an eleven-year old girl from Sarasota, Florida, walked home from a friend's house.

Carlie, a pretty girl with long blond hair, was taking a shortcut behind a carwash when a man abducted her. When she failed to return home, her family reported her missing to the Manatee County Sheriff's Office. Law enforcement responded immediately, but there wasn't a formalized response plan in place with all of the needed resources. They couldn't locate Carlie.

The following day, the carwash owner viewed the surveillance tape from the camera he had installed. The video showed a man accosting and leading Carlie away. The man wore a uniform shirt with an embroidered name patch. The carwash owner gave the tape to the police for potential evidence.

The detectives couldn't clearly read the name on the emblem. They decided to ask NASA to utilize its video enhancement equipment. However, making contact with NASA was not an easy task since its number was unlisted.

When investigators were finally able to contact NASA, they agreed to assist. As a result, police made a positive identification of this suspect that led to his capture and arrest.

Unfortunately, it was too late for Carlie. Five days later, her battered body was discovered hidden near a church parking lot about two miles from the original abduction site. The suspect ended up being convicted of Carlie's murder in November 2005, with a recommendation for the death penalty handed down by the jury.

As a result of Carlie's tragic murder, FDLE realized the importance of a rapid, organized response and how the chances of saving a kidnapped child would be enhanced. So in late 2004, they mandated every FDLE office establish a Child Abduction Response Team (CART) for missing, endangered, and/or abducted children. The CART members now had a preplanned response with a multi-jurisdictional, multi-agency, and multi-disciplined team that could immediately hit the ground running with predetermined assignments.

Upon deployment, CART members provided expertise in investigative strategies, technology, forensics, search and rescue, crime intelligence analysis, and other areas involving abducted and endangered children. This model was later adopted by the DOJ as a national model for response to a missing child.

Whereas the AMBER Alert is a tool used for public awareness and assistance in locating missing children, CART is an immediate planned response. It consists of investigators who have expertise and resources in locating abducted and endangered children.

Together, these two acronyms represent a formidable team!

Abducted from Grandma's Home

Since I was the Regional Crimes Against Children Coordinator for Southeast Florida's MROC, I was given the responsibility of developing a four-county CART program that consisted of Monroe County (Florida Keys), Miami-Dade County, Broward County (Fort Lauderdale), and Palm Beach County. We had to make sure we were in compliance with FDLE's mandate of having CART within our region.

At times, I felt overwhelmed with just the travel alone. The road mileage from Key West to North Palm Beach County is almost two hundred fifty miles of the most densely populated area of the state.

No longer was I out on the streets chasing bad boys and girls. I now spent most days saddled to an office chair and driving to the different counties. I talked on the telephone with police chiefs and sheriffs. I spent a lot of time organizing flow charts, developing resource guides, and making oral presentations to anyone who showed interest in this new crime-fighting initiative called CART.

I might have felt somewhat like a caged animal, but I was committed to this mission regardless. I knew CART's formation had the potential to help locate abducted children, and that was a huge motivator for me.

After six to eight months of a concentrated effort organizing the South Florida CART, I began to make some headway. Sheriffs and police chiefs in all four counties committed to providing their mobile command units in the area of the missing child to be used as the onsite incident command center.

Word was getting out about the CART. My growing resource list included detectives with an expertise in missing-person cases as well as search and rescue.

A lot of work had been done to pull this all together, so I decided to get away and visit my daughter Mary Ellen in Atlanta for a weekend in mid-May. While enjoying a cup of coffee on her rear deck early one beautiful Sunday morning, my cell phone rang. Early Sunday-morning phone calls from work were never good.

The caller was FDLE Special Agent Anne Estevez, who had worked with me on the Gianni Versace murder case in Miami Beach. Since then, she had transferred to the Broward field office. She had been handling some of my missing children cases while I organized the CART initiative.

Anne's voice was calm and professional. "I was called out to Lake Worth in Palm Beach County on a missing child investigation about five-thirty this morning. I'm about to go there now, but I need the CART list for resources."

I closed my eyes, wishing I could be at the scene. I was anxious about the missing child. "I'll email you the resource list ASAP. What are the details?"

"This morning during the early morning hours, Miller Neville woke up his godmother Mae Rolle. He told her three white men had burst into the unlocked home and took Miss Rolle's eight-year-old granddaughter Beverly Rolle."

"Did Beverly live with the grandmother?"

"No. She was only spending the night. According to the grandmother, the door was unlocked. She had lived in that neighborhood for years, and nothing had ever happened before. The address isn't in the best of locations, though."

I shook my head. "Who called the police?"

"The grandmother. She called at three-forty-four this morning. Two Lake Worth uniform officers responded. They conducted a hasty search of the home and surrounding area. When they didn't locate Beverly, they requested dispatch notify the on-call detective.

"The responding detective took Miller's statement. He stated he chased the men into the yard. He fought with two of them as the third guy placed Beverly into a car. The other two then jumped into the car, and they all drove away in an older model Ford."

This story seemed strange to me, but I needed to push my thoughts aside so I could give Anne the resource list.

"Great," I said sarcastically. "That narrows down the suspect list."

Anne said, "I have a hunch Miller knows more about the girl's abduction than he told us. He just didn't give that up during his interview. Anyway, the responding detective decided to call for CART, and here I am en route."

"Anne," I said, "Boca Raton Police Department has offered their mobile command unit. I'll call them and request their assistance."

"Thank you. And oh, by the way, keep your telephone and computer close by in case I need more information."

I was too far away to do anything. I felt I'd be most helpful being available for any computer assistance Anne might need, including resource information from the data I had collected and reference equipment from area police agencies that might be needed.

At that time, we didn't have the technology to send and receive emails through our phones. Anne was in the field and didn't have access to a computer, so I provided her with the information as she needed it.

Thrown Away Like Garbage

Several hours passed before Anne called again. I had been anxious, so I was glad to hear from her.

"Hey, Anne. What's the status?"

"We got her. She's alive, but barely."

I let out a sigh of relief. Although thankful they had found Beverly in time, I was still concerned about her being "barely" alive. "What happened?"

"Well, I got here the same time as the FDLE Palm Beach field office supervisor and CART members. The Boca Raton Police Department arrived with their mobile command unit not long after we got off the phone. By eight-thirty, supervisors held a briefing, and an extensive neighborhood search began.

"Floy, within minutes, the CART members located Beverly. The K-9 had followed a trail that led them right to her. Her abductor beat her, raped her, choked her into unconsciousness, and then threw her away like garbage. He tossed her head-first into a plastic recycling bin and then put that bin inside a large green dumpster in a landfill not far from the grandmother's. It gets worse."

I shook my head, my heart breaking over what had been done to this little girl. My grip on my phone tightened.

"Concrete rubble and other construction waste that weighed almost a hundred pounds had been thrown into the dumpster on top of her. At first, the cops who found her thought she was dead, but they then realized she was breathing lightly.

"She was rushed to the hospital emergency room. The doctors said her vital organs had begun to shut down. They stated she was only minutes away from death."

I had gotten tough over the years, but it didn't stop me for feeling the pain from another child tragically hurt. "Any leads on who did this to Beverly?"

"Yeah. After the search for Beverly ended, some of the detectives performed a neighborhood canvass. They came across an elderly homeless man. He had used the porch of an abandoned house across the street from the Rolle's house as shelter. He gave the detectives crucial information that helped them find Beverly's kidnapper."

Now, my heart raced with excitement. The next best news to Beverly surviving was knowing her rapist had been caught. "What happened?"

"Well, the detectives said when they talked to this homeless guy, he told them, 'I ain't seen no white guys in this hood. I did see that young fool across the street roll around in the dirt a few hours ago before the cops got here.'"

I was so glad the CART detectives had good interview skills because evidently, they were able to put the old man at ease. They respected what the old man said without judgment.

The detective re-questioned seventeen-year-old Miller Neville, their initial witness. They told him they had an eyewitness who saw him rolling on the ground to make it look like he had fought with the abductors.

What could he say? He was caught, so he confessed to the brutal attack on Beverly Rolle.

Miller Neville was sentenced to four life sentences for his despicable crime, which he is spending in a Florida prison.

"Miracle Girl"

A year later, I attended the National Missing Children's Day Ceremonies at the Department of Justice in Washington D.C. The weather was beautiful—warm and clear, white billowing clouds with a light-blue backdrop of a sky—and the sound of birds chirping.

The seven-floor building, located at 95 Pennsylvania Avenue Northwest, not only housed the Department of Justice but the U.S. Attorney General as well. More than two hundred attendees gathered together in a large auditorium for the event.

This year's ceremony was special to me because it recognized Beverly for her bravery as a child survivor. In fact, the press had dubbed her the "Miracle Girl."

Tears rolled from my eyes as I watched this precious little girl walk proudly across the stage to accept a framed document. Her big ear-to-ear smile showed off her beautiful white teeth. Pink ribbons accessorized her pigtails and a cute denim outfit with a ruffled skirt.

Everyone in attendance—federal prosecutors and law enforcement from federal, state, and local agencies from various counties—stood and clapped for this Miracle Girl.

Standing in front of my seat, I came to an important realization. All those days I had spent in my office coordinating and planning the new CART initiative for South Florida had definitely been worthwhile.

For sure, they had paid off.

A Newborn Abduction

A few months passed after that ceremony. The weather had turned hot and steamy from the calendar shifting into August.

I was in my office reviewing my extensive list of emails when Miami Beach Police Department (MBPD) Detective Jim Sharkey called me. He had been the lead detective on the Versace murder case.

"Floy, can you activate the CART? I'm standing in a seedy motel room where a new mother was badly beaten and her four-day-old infant kidnapped."

I said, "I'm on my way. I'll request the activation. Can we set up the briefing at the MBPD conference room inside the Detective Bureau?"

"Sure. I'll head over once I stop off at the hospital to check on the mother's condition."

I immediately dialed my supervisor, who then notified the SAC (Special Agent in Charge). Grabbing my suit jacket, I stuck my cell phone to my ear and kept moving. Although I had to begin the CART activation process, I couldn't waste any time. I proceeded to rush to my car while donning my jacket.

Our squad staff assistant began the member activation callout process through the Regional Highway Patrol Communications Center located in Miami.

Jim and I arrived at the same time at the MBPD. He updated me as we walked into the conference room together.

"The baby's mother Pearl Lester had moved to one of the few cheap motels located in Miami Beach. She had just given birth to her baby boy.

"She and the father Rodney are estranged. Turns out he's a charmer. He abused Pearl repeatedly. Surprise, surprise. Tallahassee also wants him for robbery of a convenience store near where he and Pearl lived together.

"When Mr. Charmer found out his girlfriend was pregnant with his child, he demanded she get an abortion. Pearl decided to keep the baby and get rid of the boyfriend instead, so she left him and relocated to live with an aunt in Miami. Rodney found her and stalked her for a month before the baby was born.

"So, Pearl checks into this motel because she was afraid Mr. Charmer would follow her to the aunt's after having the baby."

I was glad to hear that Pearl had left her abuser. Unfortunately, so many victims of domestic abuse repeatedly return to the abuser for support and/or comfort. And unfortunately, this action often results in more severe abuse or even death.

Jim looked at the report and took a few minutes to read ahead. "Rodney evidently had been watching the aunt's house. He followed her aunt to the motel where Pearl was hiding. A few minutes after her aunt drove off, Rodney kicked in the door to Pearl's motel room. He threw her on the floor and kicked her in the stomach multiple times, causing her to bleed and leaving her curled up into a fetal position."

I grimaced with the image Jim had placed in my mind. "Where was the baby when this happened?"

"The mom had him strapped into his car seat. So, when Rodney was through with Pearl, he grabbed the infant carrier that held the baby, took Pearl's car keys, and left with the baby in Pearl's car."

"Were you able to talk with Pearl at the hospital?"

"Yeah, she thinks Rodney's staying with a friend near Little Haiti."

At least we had a suspect and a possible location of where both perpetrator and baby could be. We passed this information onto CART so that members, along with the uniformed patrol officers, could saturate the Little Haiti area. They would knock on doors, visit stores and public places, and monitor the roadways and sidewalks in an effort to locate Rodney.

Two prosecutors from the Miami-Dade County State Attorney's Office arrived at the MBPD to give legal advice. They joined other members in the conference room, which had since been turned into the CART operational command center.

Four hours later, one of the CART members spotted Pearl's car travelling along a street near the aunt's house. After backup arrived, he conducted a felony car stop with his gun drawn since Rodney was a wanted violent felon.

When they approached the driver side, Rodney offered no resistance. He came across as a loving, caring father spending the day with his newborn son.

They saw the baby in his car seat. When asked where he was going, he said, "I'm taking my baby to Pearl's aunt."

Thankfully, this sweet newborn wasn't harmed.

Jim and I walked into Pearl's hospital room. The hospital was treating her for life-threatening injuries. She looked ghastly with a swollen, battered, bruised face, an eye swollen shut with a cut under it. She could hardly move.

I took her hand in mine and smiled. "We have your baby. He's safe."

Her big brown eyes focused on me. She managed to give a slight nod and smile through her pain as we both shed a tear of relief.

I said, "Pearl, your troubles with Rodney are over now. He's going away for a long time as a guest of the Florida correctional system."

Her shoulders relaxed.

I returned to the command post as the prosecutors packed up their files. Not only did they charge Rodney with auto theft, attempted murder, kidnapping, and interference with child custody, but they slapped on an additional criminal charge—burglary. Investigators had developed evidence that he had stolen the plastic infant seat.

I couldn't help but laugh.

Rescuing the Children from Monsters

A month later, FBI Special Agent Buddy Hank called me. I had last worked with Buddy on the Christmas kidnapping of the mother and her two boys.

"Floy, I'm working on an Internet luring case of a teenage girl. Will you meet me at the FBI office in Miami?"

An Internet luring case is where an adult male is chatting online with a juvenile for the purpose of manipulating her into a meeting for a sexual encounter. So, of course, I agreed.

I knocked on the doorframe to Buddy's office. He looked up at me and smiled. "Floy, great to see you again. I've heard about the CART successes and have a missing girl from Port Saint Lucie. Thought maybe you could help me with additional boots on the ground to look for this girl. Her name's Tracy, and she's only fifteen.

"Tracy has a history of running away. I was called into this case when the local police examined her computer. A forensic examination revealed she had been chatting with a registered sex offender. The sex offender lured her to meet him in Opa Locka."

I gave an involuntary squirm with this bit of news.

Buddy paused, picking up on my body language. "When I searched the sex offender's residence, I found Tracy's backpack and purse. We've interviewed the sex offender. He's in jail now for violating the conditions of his parole. He just couldn't stay away from children.

"I've conducted a neighborhood canvass and discovered that Tracy might have been sexually exploited on the streets. Can you deploy some of the CART members to double up with the Robbery Interdiction Detail that normally works Opa Locka since they know that area?"

"Yes, but since they're all at the MDPD, it's going to save time if we go on over there."

Buddy nodded in agreement. I then called some of the Miami CART members.

We arrived at the Miami-Dade Police Department just as everyone was gathering their CART packets and equipment. The briefing started early in the evening.

The CART and RID groups concentrated on all the known areas where street prostitution occurred in the Opa Locka and Liberty City areas. We decided to shut down all street prostitution as our tactic. To accomplish this feat, we would need to provide a heavy police presence by saturating the area with manpower-intensive patrol.

We ended up having so many marked and unmarked police cars roaming the street that it couldn't help but shut down business.

During the sweep, a CART officer and a RID officer discovered a thirteen-year-old girl being exploited for sex. Six weeks ago, she had been entered into NCIC as a missing child. We rescued her while trying to locate Tracy.

The streets were clear of prostitutes before the morning rush hour began. By then, the shift was ending for the members of RID and CART; they needed to get some sleep. The patrol officers were briefed about the situation and would monitor the area.

Buddy thanked me, and I headed home around six that morning to also grab some sleep.

I was still asleep when Buddy called in the early afternoon. "Tracy's mysteriously appeared on the doorstep of the Opa Locka Police Department. Someone dropped her off."

I smiled. Tracey had appeared, she was alive, and our technique was successful in getting the prostitutes out of the area. It had interfered with their pimps' income. I was very pleased all the way around!

Although Tracy was now safe, many other children continue to fall prey to traffickers, pimps, and pedophiles. These individuals don't possess a conscience. For instance, one such monster, a preferential pedophile named Oscar, liked teenage boys. He liked to lure them into his web of sexual manipulation, which consisted of kidnapping and rape.

I became aware of Oscar while investigating a missing fifteen-year-old boy. Oscar approached this child in Fort Lauderdale near a runaway shelter for teenage boys. He drew him into a hotel where he tied him up and dosed him with alcohol and drugs.

The boy woke up a day later. He found himself tied up with rope and placed in a dark room. He used his dexterity to untie himself and escape from what turned out to be Oscar's condominium in Cooper City.

This naked teenager beat on the nearby doors of frightened seniors who lived near Oscar. They subsequently called the police, and Oscar was arrested. He refused to cooperate with an interview and requested his attorney.

One of the officers who had responded to the neighbors' complaints happened to be a CART member. He knew I was looking for a male luring runaway boys to hotels with the intention of raping them. Specifically, I was attempting to locate the perp who had lured this boy to the hotel, so he called me.

"Agent Turner, the Cooper City PD has a suspect in custody they just picked up. He fits the profile of the kind of person you're looking for."

I drove immediately to the Cooper City Police Department. When I arrived, the CART member met me at the door and led me to where they were holding Oscar. He filled me in on the details of the arrest along the way.

I walked into the interview room, and the CART member introduced me to Oscar. Of course, since he had invoked his right to an attorney, I couldn't question him.

I saw a beefy fifty-year-old man with bulging brown eyes and a bulbous nose with broken blood vessels. His receding hairline led to a mixture of brown and gray strands of hair. He wore a red-and white-striped golf shirt and white Bermuda shorts. His legs displayed purple veins from his knees to his white socks. His scuffed-up, discount-store slip-on canvas shoes had bent-down heels from where he stepped on them.

I felt relieved that this case came with good news: Oscar was booked and sat in jail. His teenage victim cooperated with me. He made a statement, telling me how he was approached and where he was taken. Since he had been held hostage at Oscar's residence, he was able to identify Oscar in a lineup.

I wrote a search warrant and served it on Oscar's condo. Apparently, he lived in a pornographer's paradise. He owned volumes of sexually exploitative images of a dozen young boys. These pictures offered detailed records with the names and personal information of his victims.

I made the identifications of his other victims with the pictures and the information I had obtained during the search. My analyst conducted research on the computer to locate the other victims' addresses, schools, and such.

I requested the FDLE Crimes Against Children interview trailer, and we set it up behind the FDLE Broward field office. This thirty-five-foot mobile unit provided a child-friendly interview room with a one-way monitor for investigators who were not in the room, a workstation, and state-of-the-art audio and video equipment for capturing information.

I then interviewed the boys to verify the records and to make sure they were victims. I also enlisted help from some of the CART members who were experts in conducting child interviews.

I made good progress, building strong, solid cases using multiple victims against Oscar. Prosecutor Cathy Mueller helped me. I wanted to make sure Oscar never left the state prison system and that his victims were identified so they all could receive counseling and therapy.

In retrospect, the location of the interview trailer wasn't a secure area. The equipment was stolen out of it within a week. Welcome to South Florida!

Right after we were burglarized, Cathy called me as I was leaving the office. I felt tired after enduring a tedious day of writing memos to Tallahassee, trying to explain how FDLE became a crime victim.

Cathy sounded breathless. She began to tell me about some important information.

I thought, *I hope she's not breathless due to smoking again.* I remembered her cigarette relapse during the Nancy Goodyear investigation.

She said, "Oscar's in the hospital with sepsis. He's very ill."

I asked, "Did he catch sepsis at the jail?"

"In a way. He took a cookie off another inmate's tray in the cafeteria. The inmate hit Oscar in his face with enough force to dislodge his eye. Oscar's eye popped right out of the socket."

"Gross!"

Cathy's tone was light. "I'm on my way for a drink on Los Olas Boulevard. Want to join me?"

I was on my way home, but this new turn of events changed my mind. I thought a celebration was in order. I smiled. "See you in a few."

When I arrived, I spotted Cathy right away. She held a martini in her right hand and her cell phone up to her ear with her left hand. As soon as I sat down, she ended her call. She looked at me with a lifted eyebrow and gave a half smile. "That was the hospital calling. Oscar's dead."

Justice had been served. We needed to celebrate that none of these children would need to testify. I ordered a glass of cabernet.

We toasted to Oscar's demise.

CHAPTER NINE

BACK IN MIAMI

Gary's thirty years of undercover narcotics trafficking investigations had paid off. He received his new assignment as Special Agent Supervisor of the narcotics squad in the FDLE's Miami Regional Office.

Thank goodness, we didn't need to do any packing. Instead, we relocated our floating home from West Palm Beach to Maule Lake Marina located in North Miami Beach, just a short dinghy ride north of Biscayne Bay. This marina came with the reputation of drug smuggling during the 1970s and 1980s.

Soon after arriving, we couldn't help but notice a rustic cypress-wood handmade sign with *Smuggler's Paradise* etched on it. Someone had mounted it on an old bulkhead near the marina's entrance. Gary and I always had fun with it, joking that it made him feel at home because of his thirty years working as an undercover narcotics cop.

We loved the nautical lifestyle that was both fast-paced and laid back. It suited our personality.

Many of this marina's diverse groups of resident boaters lived on sailboats. Some, like us, dwelt on trawlers while a few others inhabited more expensive yachts. Most owned pets, such as birds, hamsters, lizards, exotic snakes, and a colorful assortment of cats and dogs of all sizes.

Our favorite new neighbors lived aboard their stunning sixty-foot aluminum Chris-Craft boat. They had rebuilt her from an almost derelict condition. This couple was fun to be around, and frequently invited us to happy hour.

Most of our neighbors cared for their vessels and kept them in superb condition. But as with every marina we had lived in, there were always owners who never cleaned the exterior or interior or their boats, and it showed. These boats looked like floating piles of junk with four-inch layers of barnacle growth that had accumulated on the hull. To make matters worse, their decks were littered with assorted broken and rusted nautical equipment and piles of unsecured dock and anchor lines.

We noticed several Corvettes parked in the marina parking lot and learned that every one of them belonged to pilots. These guys were all young and single, came from different backgrounds, and flew different aircrafts for different entities. One of the pilots worked for American Airlines, one flew a Coast Guard jet, and another flew a life flight helicopter down in the Keys.

Some of our other marina neighbors included a retired U.S. Army colonel with his wife and three cats, a single female writer who lived aboard a twenty-four-foot sailboat with her ferret, a gay couple from Colorado who both had previously been married and had kids, and a few other working folks and retirees. We relished the fact that we lived amongst such a mixture of floating Havana daydreamers who continually yearned to just float away to paradise.

As a group, boaters seemed to love the social aspect of their lifestyle, and Maule Lake Marina residents were no different. Happy hour seemed to be twenty-four hours a day due to the Jimmy Buffett rule that it's five o'clock somewhere.

Boaters took great pride in making sure that when guests came aboard their abode, they always had a cool beverage to offer. Gary and I were particularly lucky because coworkers who dropped by the boat brought their own stocked beer coolers. They wanted to ensure the beer never stopped flowing. The *C-Breeze* possessed a fifteen-foot beam-to-beam aft deck that made for the perfect relaxing atmosphere overlooking the water.

Most liveaboards also considered their dinghies sacred and kept them within easy access. On any given weekend while on the dock or out on the water, we encountered dinghies in every shape, size, and color. They were used for every sort of transportation along the water.

If a group got together and anchored their boat away from the docks, they used dinghies to roam around between the boats. Routinely, they provided entertainment for us as we raced them around the marina.

Someone always seemed to overdo it and sink one or two dinghies, but then that problem was solved rather quickly. Everyone got together, flipped it over, and got back to the task at hand, having a great time all along the way.

Back to the MROC

The marina location on the east side of Miami facilitated an easy drive for Gary's travel to work. He drove against the inbound traffic flow during the morning rush hour as he made his way to the Miami FDLE building located about fifteen miles west of the city.

As for me, my drive to the Fort Lauderdale office took about forty-five minutes to an hour, as long as the interstate wasn't blocked with accidents. I took advantage of this time, using it as an uninterrupted occasion to focus on and think through my cases.

We had been living in our new "neighborhood" for about six months when, on a Friday morning in early August, I received a telephone call from the Miami Regional Operation Center (MROC)

SAC. "Floy, I want you to move from the Broward office into the FDLE Miami headquarters to work exclusively on CART. You can select any vacant office of your choosing, and you'll be working on your own."

His announcement thrilled me. This opportunity would take me back to the Miami office where I loved to work. Plus, I would have the time I needed to complete my CART resource guides and market CART as an important tool for saving abducted or missing children.

At this point in my career, I was devoted to developing a fluid process for a functioning CART. Granted, the work may not have been as exciting as most of my prior investigative assignments, but I recognized it as an important task in achieving my goal of protecting children in harm's way.

I immediately called my husband and told him the news. He was thrilled and happy for me. Of course, he knew the move would also reduce my travel time by a lot.

Fortunately, FDLE had assigned him a pickup truck for the high waters that came from hurricanes. These destructive storms required responses from supervisors, regardless of their normal assignments.

"Gary, I need to borrow your truck so I can pack up and move my office as soon as possible. I want to get this done before the SAC changes his mind. Once I move my office, it's going to be hard for him to reverse his decision."

He said, "Floy, you don't have to move your office by yourself. I'll be happy to help you."

"Thanks. Will you do me another favor? Can you walk around the Miami FDLE building and scope out empty office spaces? I want to move this weekend."

He agreed. That afternoon, he told me about an empty office on the back side of the building.

My new office ended up having a large window, blue carpet, and a clean beige wall. I loved it.

I knew this move wouldn't involve an adjustment period. Gary and several colleagues with whom I had had the privilege to work with all had their offices in this same building. I would be able to pass them in the hallways or kitchen or other common areas. I couldn't have been happier.

By Monday morning, I had my new Miami office up and running minus any pictures on the wall. They lay on my office floor awaiting final decisions for wall placement, which would take place when Gary stopped by with a hammer and nails.

I did get a break from my desk duty. Two days after moving into my new office, North Miami Beach Detective Hal Cohen called me. I had worked with Hal during my first FDLE homicide investigation. A Florida Department of Revenue Tax Collector named Ronald Brooks had been murdered on Christmas Eve. Then later, I worked with him in the North Lauderdale abduction and rape case.

Hal said, "Floy, I need help with an investigation. I've got a child who was raped by her common-law step-grandfather when she was four. She's nineteen years old now and doesn't live in Florida anymore.

"Her rapist's name is Yan Rogerio, and he's been serving fifteen years in a Texas prison for raping another child. Now he's going to be to be released for good behavior. He's Brazilian, and he'll be deported after his release. My victim knows that wherever he goes once he's out, he'll probably victimize other children."

I was eager to help, and being back in Miami, in my element, put me closer to this case.

I said, "Sure, Hal, I'll help you."

Like this victim, I too didn't want Yan to victimize any more children in my country, or any other country for that matter. From my experience, I've never known a pedophile capable of rehabilitation.

Hal and I arranged to meet the next day and pay the grandmother a visit. She still lived in the same apartment where her granddaughter had been molested.

Interview of a Rapist in a Texas Prison

When I woke up the next morning, I went through my schedule for the day, remembering my meeting with Hal.

First things first, though. I put on a pair of shorts, a T-shirt, and sneakers and left the coolness of my boat to go outside for my morning run. The typical heat and humidity from another typical August day in Miami greeted me. Then as I ran, the heat seemed to permeate my entire being.

I took a shower afterward, but my body refused to cool down. Perspiration continued to seep through my pores, even after I stepped out of the boat's small shower and toweled off.

I decided to wear a lightweight suit with a sleeveless blouse. After dressing quickly, I donned my everyday accessories—a badge, a gun, and a pair of handcuffs, all of which were concealed under my jacket.

I climbed into my dark FDLE-issued SUV. Even before buckling my seatbelt, I cranked the air conditioner on, turning the knob to the right as far as it would go. I was met by blasts of frigid air pouring through my vents, blowing my hair away from my face. The fact that my drive to the North Miami Beach Police Department took only five minutes was of little consequence to me.

I called Hal on my way. He informed me that he was waiting for me in front of the stationhouse.

Sure enough, I saw Hal standing in front of the building's doors as I pulled into the parking lot. He looked cool and comfortable wearing a pair of designer sunglasses, a white golf shirt, and navy-blue pants. He also looked like a typical South Florida cop wearing his other accessories—a badge and a gun—clipped to his belt.

Hal climbed into my passenger seat and closed the door. He glanced at me before putting on his seatbelt. "I called and told the grandmother about our investigation. She's waiting for us at her apartment."

We drove three minutes before arriving at an older, small, and pink stucco two-story apartment building. Jalousie windows with their horizontal glass panes filled the window frames.

I parked curbside on the street under trees whose limbs extended over the sidewalk. Perfect. It would provide much-needed shade while we were gone.

Hal and I walked up to a second-floor apartment. Jalousie windows appeared to be popular with this building. Even the doors contained a long row of horizontal windows.

Hal knocked on the grandmother's door. An elderly woman opened it. She wore a black-and-white checkered, sleeveless top with a solid black skirt that ended just below her knees.

We showed her our credentials and introduced ourselves. Her solemn facial expression didn't change as she gave a brief nod and stepped aside so we could enter.

There was no foyer, just a small living room decorated with a large assortment of plastic flowers. Maybe the bright floral displays were meant to compensate for the minimal amount of furniture covered in clear plastic that sat on top of a crack terrazzo floor.

She motioned to the couch. "Please have a seat. I'm Olga Rogerio. My granddaughter told me you were going to ask me questions about Yan."

I opened my black leather portfolio case and took out a pen in preparation for taking notes. "Miss Rogerio, why do you and Yan have the same last name? It's my understanding that you've never been married."

"Yes, we were never married, but I took his last name anyway."

During the interview, Olga clearly remembered the incident when she thought Yan had molested her granddaughter. "I suspected Yan had messed with her. I remember it was close to Easter. I came in after playing bingo. Yan was holding my granddaughter on his lap with a blanket draped over her. She wasn't wearing her pajama bottoms, and she was crying. I knew something bad had happened.

"When I bathed her that night, she was irritated and bleeding from her vagina."

I wasn't surprised that Olga didn't report this horrid crime. Unfortunately, I had other encounters with caretakers of victims who chose to ignore the hard facts. They preferred to sweep the crime under the rug. Some families hid it because they felt ashamed and embarrassed and wanted to protect the family name.

She pulled her lips inward and looked down while wringing her hands. When she looked back up, her eyes were filled with tears. "Neither Yan nor my granddaughter said anything about sexual molestation at that time. Still, I told Yan to leave, and I've not seen him since. I…I didn't report any of this to the police. I'm so sorry."

Sexual assault needs to be promptly reported to the authorities to ensure the victim receives justice as well as proper therapy. If not addressed, the survivor will inevitably experience some type of acute mental, physical, or psychological issues later on. By not notifying law enforcement, the victim continues to suffer without help, and the perpetrator is free to commit evil acts on other victims.

Hal and I decided to have a visit with Yan Rogerio.

Within days, we booked a flight to Dallas. After renting a car, we drove to the nearby town where the state prison that held Yan was located.

We checked into the hotel and then looked for a nearby restaurant. We wanted to grab a quick dinner before returning to the lobby where we would strategize about tomorrow morning's interview with Yan.

Hal and I both knew we faced an uphill battle. Since Yan had been incarcerated for almost fifteen years, he had become a seasoned prisoner.

Most inmates learn from the prison grapevine how to avoid any admissions of past criminal activity to the authorities. Smart prisoners learn how to be jailhouse lawyers. They spend their time in the legal section of the prison library, studying legal decisions from other appellate cases. They receive a respected status within the prison community by providing their fellow inmates with legal advice.

As we deliberated our plan of action, we tried to predict every obstacle that could happen. First, we would need to provide Yan with his Miranda Rights before beginning an interview. We also wanted him to sign a Miranda waiver consent, a necessary form since he was in custody. Otherwise, we would be prohibited from using any statements he made for court purposes.

We knew we had to choose our words carefully to get him to sign this form. We decided to forego the formal term *interview* and chose to minimize the Miranda waiver's importance. We planned to start by telling him that we needed to get some paperwork out of the way before he could talk with us.

If Yan decided to invoke his right to an attorney, then all our efforts to obtain an interview would be in vain. The first piece of advice that any attorney gives a client is to not talk with the police.

Our interview with Yan also needed to be recorded. If he made any incriminating statements, we would have to have additional proof that he made them freely and voluntarily.

We had to take advantage of the possibility that Yan, like most prisoners, might be bored and want to play along in a cat-and-mouse game. We also hoped he felt empowered and capable of manipulating us. If so, then he'd want to be interviewed and speak to us.

After considering any and all possible hurdles, we called it a night. I went back to my room for a good night's sleep.

The next morning, we grabbed weak coffee and cold muffins. We then headed over to the prison to meet the warden before beginning our eight o'clock interview with Yan.

While walking up the sidewalk of a two-story modern building, an attractive woman with curly red hair came out to meet us. She smiled warmly. "I'm Janet Roberts. I'm the warden," she said, extending her hand. I smiled at her Texas drawl.

Warden Roberts looked to be in her fifties. Her large, green eyes accented her light complexion and freckles sprinkled over her nose.

An attractive print blouse and dark belted slacks covered her petite frame, and her flat shoes did nothing to add to her average height.

She led us into a room with small lockers lining one wall. "You can put your guns in these lockers," she instructed. She stood at the doorway and waited while we complied.

Warden Roberts then led us to her office. Family pictures gave me a feeling of warmth while the collection of coffee cups with police emblems provided a professional atmosphere. A well-organized, light-blue wooden desk sat over to one side and two blue upholstered chairs in front of it.

She sat down in a black leather executive chair behind her desk and then motioned for us to sit in the blue chairs.

She said, "I have an interview room at your disposal. We'll send Yan in when you're ready. He's my prison pastry chef." She smiled and gave a slight eye-roll, "He makes amazing cannoli."

Hal and I returned her smile. I guessed Yan's famous cannoli was fed only to the staff and not the inmates.

Warden Roberts said, "I'll be here all day. When you finish your interview, please stop back in before you go."

She picked up her telephone receiver asked for a guard to come escort us inside the prison to the interview room.

While the guard took Hal and me through the quiet building, I became impressed with its out-of-the-norm characteristics. Not a smudge could be found on its light-gray walls. The floors looked clean and waxed to a high gloss. We learned that a private corporation owned this prison and contracted with the state.

Hal and I entered the large interview room. More gray walls with polished green floors contained a composite wood desk and three gray metal chairs—very sparse but spotless. We decided to arrange the furnishings to make a comfortable setting to our advantage.

First, we pushed the table back against the wall and set our recorder and portfolios on it. We took the chairs and placed them in a circle, omitting any barriers. We stood, awaiting our guest.

A few minutes later, Yan entered the room wearing a white shirt, white pants, and dark shoes. A tall white chef's hat topped his gray hair, giving a little more height to his short and heavy build. His wrinkled skin showed his age, and his ashen complexion revealed years of being inside. I could smell the aroma of pastries emitting from his clothing, and I noticed a small sprinkling of what looked like flour on the top of his shoes.

Since we had asked the prison not to notify him of our visit, he seemed curious as he looked us up and down.

Yan removed his hat. "Where are you cops from?'

Hal took the lead. "North Miami Beach."

Yan suddenly changed facial expressions. The wrinkles around his brows increased as his eyes widened.

Hal motioned to the small circle of chairs with his hand. "Yan, take a seat."

The three of us sat down almost simultaneously. I held the pen and paper in my hands for my note taking.

Hal said, "Yan, I'm going to use a recorder during our conversation."

Yan froze for a moment when he heard Hal mention a recorder. His initial relaxed facial muscles became tense, and his eyes narrowed some. His guarded expression didn't give me a good vibe.

Hal tried to break the ice and get Yan to open up with us. He asked him about his job as a pastry chef, complimenting him on what the warden had told us about his cannoli.

We sat in the interview room with Yan for hours. He didn't sign the Miranda consent form. We gave our best efforts, but in the end, we didn't come close to a confession. Yan only wanted to talk about how he perfected his recipe for his cannoli.

After six and a half hours, we finally conceded defeat. I called the guard, and we walked back to the warden's office.

The warden handed us a brown paper bag. "Here's your Johnny sack."

When she used this term, I knew she meant "snack" from when I had escorted prisoners for the U.S. Marshal's Office. I learned that the Texas prisons called a brown paper bag with bologna or peanut butter and jelly sandwiches "Johnny sacks."

Hal was clueless. A Jewish boy from New York transplanted to Miami had never heard that term.

The warden smiled. "I put a cannolo in each bag."

Both Hal and I felt emotionally drained. My empty stomach turned at the thought of bologna and cannoli.

Warden Roberts also presented us with the traditional blue coffee mug gift. The prison name was embossed in gold lettering on the front.

We both thanked her for allowing us to interview Yan and for our departing gifts. When we turned to leave, I noticed that Hal's red eyes and frown made him look as dejected as I felt. We needed a drink.

All of a sudden, the warden laughed. "The hell with this! Throw those sacks away. I'm closing my office and taking you both out for some Texas barbeque and longneck bottles of beer."

Warden Janet Roberts possessed a cop humor which we needed. It lifted our spirits.

I didn't have the heart to tell her I didn't drink beer. I took one for the team, though. I must admit that on that afternoon, the Texas beer tasted great.

I took comfort in knowing this case wasn't over. We had the victim's statement, a very detailed account of her rape to Hal before he had even called me. The grandmother had also provided collaboration. Still, obtaining a confession was always best for court.

Hal and I convinced the Miami-Dade County State Attorney's Office to file charges against Yan. They included a detainer for when he would get released from Texas custody. This would keep him at the Texas prison for the next eight months or so, common when awaiting charges in another jurisdiction.

Finally, the time came when the NMBPD picked up Yan and transported him to the jurisdiction of his crime—Miami. After returning to the Miami-Dade County Jail, he realized it was in his best interest to accept a plea agreement of seven years in a Florida prison. If he went to trial, he knew he could get a life sentence.

After he completed his seven years, he would be deported to Brazil. Unfortunately, once he was outside of the U.S., he wouldn't be registered as a sex offender.

Maybe someday, persons convicted of these horrible crimes will be tagged wherever they go in the world. That would be a good thing.

Hurricane Katrina

I went back to work on my CART duties. I believed we needed further development for CART training, so I decided to offer our members training on interviewing sex offenders.

I expected over eighty participants to attend the two-day training, so I reserved the largest room in the Miami FDLE headquarters. The national expert I requested to conduct the training happened to be an FDLE Special Agent who had traveled from Tallahassee to Miami to speak at this event.

All went fine until the first afternoon. I learned that the hurricane in the Atlantic Ocean had changed direction and threatened South Florida. The room I had been using transformed into the Emergency Operations Center for the FDLE Miami Region, forcing me to cancel Day Two of the training. We moved out of the room as the tech agents brought in extra telephones and computers to manage the storm response.

My speaker joined Gary and me on the aft deck of our boat. He was our friend and not scheduled to leave until the next morning, so we threw him an impromptu farewell party that night. He kept the party going, and the rum flowed.

In reality, a dual purpose existed for his trip. After the training, he planned to take the Crimes Against Children Mobile Interview trailer back to Tallahassee. They could then complete the repairs on the damage caused by the burglary that happened behind the Broward Field Office.

When the party ended, the calm wind and still air signified what boaters called "the calm before the storm." By the time my speaker got up, packed, and hooked up the trailer, the winds were kicking up. He needed to get out of "Dodge," and quickly.

On August 23, 2003, Hurricane Katrina loomed out of the Atlantic and started heading our way. Gary and I prepared to secure all the boat lines, adding multiple sets on all sides.

We decided to stay onboard during this storm to manage the dock lines as the tide changes occurred. The tides could very well double or triple above normal during a storm. We had both observed many poorly secured boats ripped apart and sunk during storms when owners left them unattended.

On August 25, the eye of Katrina crossed directly over us. Thankfully, it had not yet escalated from a category-one status.

During the storm, I spent hours on the deck in eighty-mile-per-hour winds, holding a large fifteen-inch rubber boat bumper between the dock and our boat's hull and wishing I was anyplace else.

At the same time, Gary was busy with the boat docked next to us. Its owner was in Texas, and both aft lines on his boat had snapped, becoming a hazard and endangering both of our boats. They could be thrown against each other, break free, and damage or sink other nearby vessels. Plus, everyone in the marina looked after each other's boat.

Gary started the engines so the propellers would keep the boat from hitting the seawall. We also had to keep both boats off the pilings and from banging into the concrete. Gary focused on our neighbor's boat while I kept our boat secure by making sure the bumper stayed in place.

Being onboard a boat during a category-one hurricane, even as large as our seventeen-ton trawler, turned out to be quite unpleasant. I must admit I felt nervous at the high waves and the boat's tossing and turning and shaking violently all night.

Little Bit hated it the most. I needed to give her doggie motion-sickness pills. I even considered taking a few myself.

Living aboard a self-contained boat had its upside. When living in a house on land, you could lose electricity during a hurricane, sometimes for weeks at a time. On a boat, though, you only needed to touch the generator's button, and voila, you had all the necessary luxuries of home: lights, TV, air conditioning, cold beer, and best of all, a warm shower at the end of the day.

However, the Gulf Coast and New Orleans didn't fare as well as us. They didn't even have the opportunity to use generators. Four days later, these areas experienced Katrina's devastation when it picked up greater strength crossing the warm, open waters of the Gulf of Mexico. It hit the southeast Louisiana coast as an extremely destructive hurricane.

Memories of losing my home in Hurricane Andrew deluged my mind. I grieved with these folks. I felt their pain and loss and understood it too well. However, the intensity and degree of flooding experienced by New Orleans was worse.

Immediately following the hurricane, Gary and his squad were dispatched to work for a couple of weeks along the Mississippi coast. In the meantime, Hurricane Katrina refugees from New Orleans fled to Florida. The Palm Beach Polo Club served as a shelter for its victims. FDLE had also organized an effort to identify and locate any missing children who might have made their way to our state.

Although I had returned to work and resumed my normal duties, I felt as if it wasn't enough. Here were families who had suffered through extreme devastation, and I wasn't doing anything to help. I couldn't sit by and simply hear about what these victims were going through anymore. I called Tallahassee and offered my assistance.

A few days later, Tallahassee asked me to interview a set of parents who could not locate their children. I drove from Miami to Palm Beach where I was introduced to the parents, Freddy and Lolly Jackson. The incident upset Freddy so much that he had been briefly hospitalized for stomach pains.

The parents told me that before Katrina struck the Ninth Ward, the area where they lived, they had taken their three children to the home of Lolly's mother. They felt that since her home was further away from the water, their children would be safer.

Freddy spoke softly. "After dropping them off, me and Lolly went back to our house to board it up and get our stuff. But when the hurricane made landfall, water started flooding our first floor. We went up to the attic and stayed there throughout the storm. When the hurricane died down, we opened the attic door and saw lots of water. We knew the entire neighborhood had flooded, so we climbed up on our roof.

"Then I saw a boat floating in the water. We climbed down the house, and I put Lolly in it and pulled her through the water for many blocks. The water was filled with mud and all kinds of things from the storm."

Freddy gave a shudder as tears filled his eyes. "While I was pulling the boat to safety, bodies floated by."

Lolly's eyes also contained pools of tears. "We finally made our way to my mother's house. It had been badly damaged. No one knew what happened to our family."

I was completely immersed in the retelling of their tragedy, my heart breaking for them. I reached over and handed them tissues.

I asked, "How did you get here?"

At this point, Freddy was about to break down. Lolly glanced over at him, her eyebrows rising with concern. She then looked back at me. "The Coast Guard picked us up and flew us here to Palm Beach County."

I asked, "Have you heard any word about the grandmother and your children?"

They both shook their heads. Lolly's eyes pleaded with me to help while Freddy continued to look down.

I took all the pertinent information about Freddy, Lolly, the grandmother, and the children. Freddy had the children's school records but not their birth certificates.

I touched Lolly's hand and leaned into them. "I promise I'll be diligent in trying to locate your children."

According to the Department of Justice, missing children fall into one of four categories: nonfamily abductions, family abductions, runaways/throwaways, or lost, injured, or otherwise missing (LIM). In a mass catastrophe like Katrina, children who are separated from their caretakers fall under the last category.

I began a long series of telephone calls to the New Orleans Police Department. They were in crisis mode and overworked with so many emergency calls. No one could help me.

I then called the National Center for Missing and Exploited Children (NCMEC). They gave me a contact number for a Team Adam member assigned to the Louisiana's Superdome, where those who had lost their homes were sent.

Team Adam members were employed by NCMEC as consultants because they possessed expertise in missing and abducted children investigations. They had already travelled to New Orleans where they assisted with the missing-children issue.

Through Team Adam, I tracked the missing children to the Superdome and developed a timeline for the children's movements, starting at the grandmother's house. During a disaster where most of the infrastructure had been disrupted, this task became difficult to accomplish.

Team Adam also helped me locate the grid to which they had initially been assigned. I found the grandmother but not the kids.

Because the results didn't match the paperwork and the information from my phone calls, I proceeded to call the Red Cross. Of course, they were overwhelmed with this crisis, and my phone calls kept going into their voicemail. On about my twentieth try, I finally reached a live person—a Red Cross member who gave me valuable information. The conditions inside the Dome had become so bad due to no power, no working sanitation, and poor management, the grandmother's assigned section had been evacuated to Houston's Astrodome.

Finally, after three days of hard work, I felt like I had a lead that could produce positive results. I called the Houston Police Department (HPD), and they too were swamped. They had been assigned control over the refugees at the Astrodome.

My persistence paid off, however. After the fifth or sixth attempt at calling them, I was able to speak to a supervisor in the emergency command center. Fortunately, they possessed meticulous records.

HPD contacted an officer assigned to the Astrodome. After six and a half hours, he located the grandmother and then immediately called me so that I could speak with her. She said the children were with her, and they were safe.

I let out a sigh of relief, not realizing that it had been pent up inside me all this time. However, I wasn't done.

Now I needed to reunite the children and their parents. This family was destitute, and they had no money to spend on flight tickets. I spent the next couple days on the phone looking into a variety of programs that were both government and nonprofit. I wasn't successful in getting financial help to fly the parents to Houston to pick up their children.

My supervisor shared another concern. The parents didn't have their children's birth certificates or other proof that they had legal custody of their children. They only had school records.

I didn't like hearing this obstacle, although I knew he had a strong point. I felt comfortable that these were their children and that they needed to brought to Florida. I had looked into their eyes as I interviewed them. It was a gut feeling.

The parents had touched my heart. I grieved and worried alongside them, so much so that I became obsessed in reuniting this family.

To placate my supervisor, I conducted criminal histories on both Freddy and Lolly in NCIC. Two prior misdemeanor charges and convictions for marijuana showed up on Freddy's report. He was credited with time served. Lolly didn't have any criminal charges or convictions.

Armed with this information, I walked into my boss's office, confident in my decision to move forward. I just needed to pass it onto him.

He smiled when he saw me. I decided to get straight to the point. "We need to get this family back together. If we wait for New Orleans to give us copies of the children's birth certificates, it could take months. I believe Freddy and Lolly are the parents. I've confirmed with the grandmother that the parents have custody."

Admittedly, I only had this woman's confirmation over the telephone of who she was and who the children were. I realized that I had just voluntarily placed my head on the chopping block. I prayed for discernment and that no issues from this decision would bite me later on.

I happened to mention this situation to my dear girlfriend Treva, a nurse in the hospital's Newborn Intensive Care Unit (NICU). She came up with a solution.

She knew a pediatrician who had practices in both South Florida and South America. The doctor owned a jet that he used to travel to and from his practices.

My heart raced. I thought, *Wow! How cool is this perfect solution?*

My friend asked the doctor about assisting with the transportation of the Jackson family. He willingly offered the use of his plane to fly the parents from Boca Raton to Houston and back. What a generous man.

When I notified FDLE with these arrangements, they put up no resistance at all. We still weren't at the finish line yet, but we were getting there.

I needed to go on the plane and make sure the pickup was smoothly executed and without any delays. Since this mission cost a lot of money with two private pilots on the doctor's payroll, I had a responsibility to make sure the entire mission went off without a hitch.

I then realized that the best thing was for me to stay put and continue coordinating all the agencies from my phone as well as be available should some issue crop up at the last minute. I had been working the phones all along and developed rapports with those I had spoken to. I knew I needed to continue making contacts via telephone. Being at the office allowed me to strategize to keep this tactical operation fluid and make sure it all came together. Thankfully, FDLE Special Agent Anne Estevez stepped up and offered to fly to Houston with the parents.

When the day and time arrived for the flight, no one paid attention to the intense heat. None of us had anything else on our minds except reuniting this family.

Anne drove to the airport and parked her car. I picked up the parents and drove them to meet Anne and the plane at Boca Raton Signature Airport.

We walked into the airport's exclusive Signature Lounge. Its exquisite ambiance with shiny marble floors and leather lounge chairs served to put everyone into a great frame of mind. Don't even get me started on its fancy bathrooms stocked with every possible amenity from mouthwash to expensive creams.

These parents had only flown once in their lives, and that was the Coast Guard flight out of New Orleans that had brought them here to

Palm Beach. Now they had moved up to a private jet. Their excitement and anticipation at being reunited with their children trumped their travel nerves as demonstrated by their perpetual smiles.

Freddy sat in one of the comfy chairs. Lolly swayed and pranced around the room as if she were dancing to music in her head; she was so happy.

They all boarded. I stayed and watched until the time of "wheels up."

I drove to the Fort Lauderdale office. Since it would provide a quiet place to make my calls on my cell phone, I saw no reason to drive to Miami only to drive back to pick up the group.

I checked in with my contact in Houston, a sergeant with the police department. He said, "We have one problem."

My heart sank while my pulse quickened. "What?"

"When I got to the Astrodome, I discovered the section where the Jacksons were assigned had been moved."

"Use the PA!" I pleaded. "You've got to find those kids!"

The sergeant said, "There's a lot of noise inside there, and it's hard to hear any announcements."

Thoughts raced through my mind as if trying to keep up with my racing heart. "Get the Red Cross and everyone to find them. I can't have a jet sitting with two pilots and no children."

Total panic took over my entire being as I hung up. At this point, I could only pray, and pray I did.

Within an hour, the sergeant called back. He sounded calm. "I'm driving to the airport to pick up the Jacksons and your agent. All is well. We located the Jackson family. They'll be standing in front of the Astrodome for the reunification."

I could literally feel my heart rate decrease. I let out a slow breath, thanking God for answering my prayers.

All went well after the initial hiccup.

By late afternoon, the flight was "wheels down" at the Boca Raton Airport. I sat in my car on the tarmac, watching a flawless landing. I was beyond ecstatic.

The ground crew put the wood blocks in front of the tires and rolled out the red carpet. I got out of my car just in time to see the door open and the Jacksons, Anne, and the pilots exit the plane.

We all posed for a picture, which was placed in the FDLE newspaper *The Informant*.

Now that the Jackson family was reunited, they decided it was time for Freddy and Lolly to marry. My girlfriend Ann Marie, who owns a bridal shop in Homestead, dressed Lolly at the Polo Club. My pastor from the First Presbyterian Church in Boynton Beach officiated the wedding service.

Unfortunately, Anne Estevez had to miss the wedding. The kids had colds when they got on the plane in Houston. Not only was Anne blessed to be part of picking up the kids and bringing them home, but she also picked up a terrible cold and fever and brought it home with her as well.

She missed a joyous time. Lolly was a beautiful bride, and she, Freddy, and the children looked so elated as they started their life together as one big happy family.

CHAPTER TEN

NEW TERRITORY

Gary accepted the position of Special Agent Supervisor in the Jacksonville Regional Operations Center (JROC). The timing was good since I planned to retire within sixteen months; the location was beneficial because I got to be closer to my daughter and our precious new twin grandchildren in Atlanta.

As an additional perk, the FDLE offered me a position in its Saint Augustine field office, which was considered part of the Jacksonville region.

One downside would be the culture shock I would probably experience. I had grown accustomed to the hustle and bustle of a large metropolitan city, and I loved the diversity of Miami. The small, laid-back historical city of Saint Augustine, though, would be an adjustment for me.

Furthermore, I didn't want to lose the relationships I had developed over the years with many law enforcement and judicial colleagues from a variety of local, state, and federal agencies all over South Florida. I would have to start over so close to retirement.

Another downside would be my need to resign from my position as the Regional Crimes Against Children Coordinator since I was leaving the region. Understandably, this new endeavor gave me some trepidation, despite the family benefits.

Before the big transition, Gary and I took a road trip up to the Jacksonville area. We scoped out marinas since we were once again moving our floating home. We quickly realized that living in

Northeast Florida would be different in location and commute time as well. We decided to relocate to a marina in Green Cove Springs, a small town along the Saint Johns River coast. It was about halfway between Gary's job and my job—a thirty-minute drive to work for me and a fifty-minute drive for Gary.

At least when we moved, we didn't have to worry about moving our vehicles. We had already moved our personal vehicle a few weeks before our boat. Our other ones belonged to the state. We returned them to their proper owners, knowing we would be assigned new vehicles once we arrived in North Florida.

On a cool and windy morning in January 2006, we departed Miami to make our trek to North Florida. Little Bit and I stood on the bow and watched as the waves lapped against *C-Breeze*'s hull.

I felt overwhelmed as I saw my neighbors lined along the dock to see us off and wave goodbye. I wiped away tears while I stowed the dock lines and bumpers on deck, placing the boat in cruise-ready mode.

To make this journey fun and deflate the dismal atmosphere of the pending change, we decided to make our departure into a party, especially since another couple joined us for the first few days of our travel. They wanted to learn more about traveling by trawler and the lifestyle that accompanied it.

Gary and I knew the couple from working with them at FDLE. We had also participated in some off-duty activities together, so we anticipated a fun time aboard.

Within thirty minutes of departure, our first "bump in the road" surfaced. Gary noticed the boat's helm had quit responding to the steering.

I watched him, looking for any sign in his body language that we were good to go. Instead, his eyebrows were furrowed in concern. Not being able to steer the boat could be a big problem as we went up the Intercoastal Waterway. Gary put her on autopilot.

I completely trusted Gary's ability to captain our boat under any circumstance, but the idea that we had lost most of our steering control caused me some apprehension.

Throughout the first day, Gary made multiple trips into the engine room to inspect every aspect of our steering components. He couldn't isolate exactly what was causing the problem.

We ended up stopping early the first afternoon and dropping anchor just off the channel. We all settled in to watch a beautiful multi-colored sunset on the waterway.

After a few more days without complete steering control, we decided to spend a full day at a marina with its own repair shop on site. It felt good to get off the boat, find a good restaurant, and buy a few new groceries. We also said goodbye to our friends as they headed back to South Florida. From this point on, it was just Gary, Little Bit, and me.

Gary figured out that the *C-Breeze*'s steering issues came from losing hydraulic fluid, yet he couldn't determine where the leak was coming from. Continuing to add new fluid two to three times each day provided us with partial helm response.

Admittedly, the combination of leaving behind what I'd known for decades and the steering issue made the trip more unsettling than I wanted.

This issue continued to plague us as we moved north through the Intercoastal. We didn't feel comfortable taking our boat too far offshore and into the ocean. We also needed to move at a slower speed in the Intercoastal, all of which caused the trip to take an extra day. The most challenging areas turned out to be maneuvering in shallow and narrow channel waters close to inlets with a strong tidal current.

On our last full day of cruising, we encountered heavy morning fog as *C-Breeze* departed Beach Marina just north of Saint Augustine. We continued north to Jacksonville because that was the only way we could access the Saint Johns River. We would then travel south to our destination.

The thick fog kept Gary from seeing me as I stood vigil at the bow to warn him of any channel markers and dangerous situations like nautical debris and nearby vessels. Consequently, we needed total concentration and trust in the radar screen to avoid a collision or run aground. These conditions forced us to move at only three knots, so we anticipated a very long day ahead of us. Finally, at about ten in the morning, the fog moved out, and we could finally see the Jacksonville skyline.

Seeing the bridges and buildings was nice, but we couldn't celebrate yet. We still needed to navigate through town and further inland.

Dealing with the fog turned out to be a good thing. It took our minds off the poor steering response since we had to move so very slow.

The boat seemed to navigate easier with the strong incoming tides of the Saint Johns River. Gary shouted that *C-Breeze* was registering speeds close to fourteen knots as we made our way through the strong currents near the city.

Late that day, just as the cool January sun began to set, we moved slowly into our new marina dock near Green Cove Springs. We settled into our new community and celebrated by sharing multiple glasses of wine and many cold beers with our new neighbors as we reconstructed events of our trip.

Boaters always love to hear stories about a good adventure on the water.

A Farewell to a Hero, a Warrior, and My Friend

Now we needed to get back to work.

I would still occasionally be called to supplement the governor's protective security detail. No longer the Crimes Against Children Coordinator, I was now assigned to a wide variety of investigations.

The Saint Augustine field office SAC knew my heart was in CART, and the supervisor running CART was glad to let me focus on it. Jacksonville already had a CART, but I offered to take responsibility for a three-county team that fell under the Saint Augustine field office. I ended up reorganizing and regionalizing them as three separate CARTs under the JROC.

Once I got its CART program up and running, I decided to create a mock abduction field training exercise. It turned out to be the first national CART mock-abduction field-training exercise in the U.S. Over two hundred members of the Northeast Florida CART participated in this event that covered Saint Johns, Putnam, and Flagler counties.

Law enforcement CART members from all over the state traveled to observe this training exercise. The news media focused on the exercise activities, and the three major Jacksonville news stations highlighted the drill in their daily broadcasts.

Shortly afterward, Karen Kool called to say she happened to be in my area and wanted to have lunch. We spent the first part of our time together catching up, laughing, and joking around with each other. Then her smile left her face, and her eyebrows pulled up in the middle. I thought I caught a glimpse of fear when she opened her eyes wide for a split-second.

She looked down and folded her hands on the table. Her voice cracked when she spoke. "Floy, I'm in town because I had to go to Mayo Clinic for a medical evaluation. I've been diagnosed with an autoimmune illness, and I have to go on medical leave. I won't be able to work in the field again as an FBI Agent anymore."

I was stunned but tried not to show it. It was hard to hold back the tears. Honestly, I didn't know what to say, so all I could do was silently pray.

The light-hearted mood had changed. We were warriors, tough cops who had spent a lifetime battling evil, so we did what cops typically do when facing personal devastation: we pushed aside her words to get our minds off of the issue, if only for a while. We resumed our conversation about the cases we had worked together.

After lunch, she drove back to Miami while I drove back to my office. My heart felt heavy. Karen had become a dear friend and colleague to me over the years. Our cases flashed before me, and I couldn't help but smile at the many victories we achieved together. We both had been so tenacious in getting justice, and I had known that I could always count on her and vice versa.

I admired her tremendously. She had never married; her fidelity belonged to the FBI, and her only children were her adopted dogs. I recalled her telling me how she had started off in the Bureau as an FBI pilot. She had to crash one of its planes in the ocean off Key West due to engine failure. She swam in those waters until she reached shore.

I preferred to believe the best for Karen, that she would be okay, but my belief was short-lived. Over the next few months, we spoke frequently over the phone, but her voice was getting weaker, and I knew her health was failing.

Karen soon passed away. I felt as if I had been punched in my heart. I cried and mourned her loss, for the FBI, for the children she was so passionate to protect, for me and our friendship, and for this world who lost a true hero and warrior.

I know she is at peace.

Life and the Badge

Not long after my friend's death, I sat in my office looking out the window at the bright Florida sun. Karen came to my mind. For a brief moment, I swore I saw her reflection in the glass, smiling back at me, and I allowed a couple of tears to fall.

Memories of Karen, our working together, and our friendships flooded my mind. I recalled when Karen brought her two bloodhounds to the Fort Lauderdale FDLE office to show them off to the agents. She kept a towel with her to constantly wipe the drool off their snouts.

I smiled at the sweet memories. Fortunately, an FBI supervisor adopted them after she passed.

I remembered our lunches and dinners together over the years, how we "got" each other and our commitment to our job and to the children, her valuable input on our cases, how we talked on the phone for hours about them, and our trips together. Undoubtedly, she was an advocate for justice, but she was taken from this earth way too soon.

I thought about all the other friends I had lost since becoming a cop. I realized more than a couple of tears had fallen, and I wiped them away with the back of my hand.

To overcome this sadness, I thought about all the wonderful friends who were still with me, some close by while others lived hundreds of miles away. I knew I could also count on them in the most dangerous and life-threatening circumstances. Some were friends for a short season before moving on while others remained friends for a lifetime.

I reflected on my career. In a few months, I would be retiring and closing this lengthy chapter of my life. Admittedly, I had mixed feelings about leaving. One moment I was excited, knowing I could do whatever I wanted whenever I wanted. The next moment I was sad, and yes, at times, scared. Law enforcement had been my life for the past twenty-five years.

Leaving law enforcement wasn't like leaving a corporate job. To me, law enforcement wasn't a job; it wasn't even a career. Law enforcement was a lifestyle. You and the badge became one, and it came to a point where you didn't know where one started and the other ended.

Bonds were formed that could never be broken, bonds created from knowing someone had your back when no one else did; bonds created from surviving life-and-death situations together; bonds created from knowing that other person got you because he or she walked in the same shoes you did, felt the same fear you did when looking pure evil in the eye, the same joy when seeing people overcoming the odds and becoming victorious through the most horrendous of circumstances, and the same satisfaction when justice was served.

I thought about the many cases I had participated in and investigated, from my crazy escapades as a Florida Highway Patrol Trooper and the many drugs we took off the street, to the high-level criminal investigations as a Florida Department of Law Enforcement Special Agent and the serial murderers, kidnappers, rapists, predators, and the like we had put away after months of hard work. Admittedly, we hadn't been able to catch them all, but it wasn't for lack of trying.

I took satisfaction in knowing I had been part of making a huge dent in the world of crime. I could walk away knowing I had upheld my oath to serve and protect to the best of my ability. I could leave behind a legacy that would help abducted children all over the country. I didn't think I could leave on a better note.

My life behind the badge had changed me, I believe for the better. I'm convinced no other job could have impacted me more. Through it, I truly learned about human nature, the good, the bad, and the ugly. I walked away knowing that ultimately, most people are good. That knowledge comforted me.

I allowed myself to indulge in my bittersweet memories before being interrupted by a bird that flew by my window just inches from the pane. I watched it fly away, and I imagined its carefree life with no worries except to eat. It probably never had to prove itself in a man's world at a time when a woman needed to prove her abilities physically, mentally, and emotionally before she could be accepted as a competent colleague and comrade. Although wearing a badge for female cops at that time was uncommon and unpopular, the initial lack of acceptance toughened me.

If I had to do it all over again, would I again choose to break that glass ceiling, to permeate the thin blue line with my femininity and be a woman in law enforcement? You betcha!

After all, there was never really a choice. I would always be a cop, proudly standing firm behind the thin blue line.

Being a cop was my destiny; it was part of my DNA because being a cop was what God created me to be.

AFTERWORD

Upon my retirement from the FDLE in 2007, I continued to advocate for children.

I became a consultant, and I served in various capacities for the Office of Justice AMBER Alert Program, assisting with curriculum development, training law enforcement, and serving as the AMBER Alert Liaison for the Eastern U.S. and Caribbean. I had the privilege of working with some of the most dedicated groups of consultants to be found anywhere.

Later on, the Department of Justice AMBER Alert Program incorporated my CART operations and training model nationally for agencies seeking CART certification. Using this program would show them how to meet the organizational standards that needed to be recognized when a child went missing.

As I traveled throughout the United States, I met and worked with wonderful police officers and victim advocates. Their diligence in seeking justice for those who didn't have a voice of their own impressed me.

I was then selected to serve as an instructor for the Organization of American States in combating human trafficking throughout the Caribbean and Central and South America. This human-rights issue had just begun to gain recognition as a true worldwide problem for these victims.

We've only scraped the surface. So much still needs to be accomplished in combating human trafficking before this injustice can be eliminated. I pray that one day our world will be free of slavery and that all human beings can coexist in peace.

My professional life post-retirement seemed to be soaring, but my personal world got rocked to the core when in 2009, Gary was diagnosed with pancreatic cancer. After undergoing intensive surgeries, I'm happy to announce that Gary survived and is currently cancer-free. We've been blessed with great medical care and a strong support system.

In 2013, I left the Office of Justice, thinking I would retire for good, but it hasn't worked out that way. I served on the board of directors for Quigley House, Clay County's domestic-violence shelter and sexual-assault center, and I served as the interim president for the Florida Missing Children's Day Foundation for almost two years. In addition, I became an international consultant for the International Center for Missing and Exploited Children, conducting training on human trafficking and missing and abducted children for police, prosecutors, child protection workers and investigators, and NGOs (Non-Government Organizations). I've also received an appointment from FDLE Commissioner Richard Swearingen as a member of the Florida Department of Law Enforcement Missing Endangered Persons Information Clearinghouse Advisory Board.

Gary and I live in South Florida. I continue to serve as a volunteer with the Indian River County Sheriff's Office where I assist in their CART program.

Little Bit passed on, and our black Lab, Macon, has eased the healing of that loss. We're enjoying and appreciating life together more than ever. In fact, we spend most of our mornings working out in the gym. Gary plays Pickleball, and I take yoga classes.

We have lived an adventure-filled life, and all along the way, we continued to stand firm in our faith in God. It has kept us in the tough times and made the good times that much better.

Our lives would not have been as fulfilling if not for our love for each other, from great friends and family, and a true love for life that we learned to appreciate that much more as a result of the badge.

FLOY TURNER

In April 2007, Floy Turner retired as a special agent from the Florida Department of Law Enforcement after serving as the Regional Crimes Against Children Coordinator in the Miami Region of Southeast Florida.

Her investigative assignments have included complex investigations of serial homicide, kidnapping, missing children, child homicide, and human trafficking cases. She has served as a member of an Internet Crimes Against Children Task Force, the Law Enforcement Against Child Harm (LEACH) Task Force, the Miami-Dade County and Broward County Child Death Review Boards and U. S. Immigration and Customs Enforcement Human Trafficking Task Force.

Turner was responsible for establishing a Child Abduction Response Team (CART) for the South Florida Region. She also developed a three-county CART in the St. Augustine area. She assisted in the development of the Human Trafficking curriculum for Basic Law Enforcement Training and Incentive Classes for Florida Police Officer's Standards.

In 2004, Turner was awarded the State Law Enforcement Officer of the Year at Florida Missing Children's Day. From 2006 to 2012, she was employed as a consultant on the development and implementation of various training initiatives for an Office of Justice Program, the National AMBER Alert Training and Technical Assistance Program. She served as the AMBER Alert Liaison for the Eastern United States and Caribbean. Turner created the Child Abduction Response Team (CART) Certification program, which included a mock child abduction exercise. She was appointed by Governor Crist to the Florida Statewide Task Force on Human Trafficking in 2010.

From 2010 to 2013, Turner was selected by the Organization of American States to conduct human trafficking training for government officials throughout the Caribbean and South America. From 2016 to present, Turner has been consulting with the International Center for Missing and Exploited Children as an international trainer. She also serves on the advisory board of Florida Department of Law enforcement's missing endangered persons clearinghouse.

Turner received her bachelor of liberal studies degree from Barry university. She was awarded the 2016 John and Reve' Walsh Award at the Florida Missing Children's Day. In 2018, Floy was appointed to the Florida Department of Law Enforcement Missing Endangered Persons Information Clearinghouse Advisory Board.

Recently, Turner has co-authored the two best-selling books, ***Behind Her Miami Badge*** and ***Behind Her Special Agent Badge***. The sequel to ***Behind Her Criminal Investigator's Badge***.

SHERRIE CLARK

SHERRIE CLARK is the co-author of the best-selling books *Behind Her Miami Badge* and its sequel *Behind Her Special Agent Badge* and the author of the best-selling book *Small Voices Silenced*, which is her memoir. Through her unique creative writing style, she brings reality to stories by putting readers in the shoes of the characters so that they can experience what the characters see, hear, and feel.

Sherrie's reputation in ensuring quality for her clients has caused her to be a sought-after ghostwriter, author coach and consultant, book editor, book publisher, and speaker. With many of the books she works on, she draws from her past experiences as a NYPD police officer and Licensed Clinical Christian Counselor through NCCA.

As the CEO of Storehouse Media Group (StorehouseMediaGroup.com) and co-owner of Book Concept 2 Best Seller (BookConcept2BestSeller.com), she works with busy and aspiring authors to pull out stories and messages and craft them in a way that gives her clients credibility and value.

She loves to share her expertise and knowledge, so she educates authors through conferences and online classes on how to write their books in a simple step-by-step, tried and proven formula and then how to develop them to page turners.

Before tackling books, Sherrie started writing copy in 2004 and still continues to do so, applying her seasoned skills acquired through both years of experience and ongoing training. Her clients have consisted of businesses, entrepreneurs, attorneys, high-tech companies, non-profit organizations, and authors. Consequently, she's a proud member of the Professional Writers' Alliance.

As a visionary, she knew in late 2012 that podcasts were the wave of the future. Armed with her involvement of working with victims, she created, produced, and hosted the live weekly podcast *God, Where Were You When?* that became part of Lester Sumrall's LeSEA Broadcasting Network.

Sherrie has enjoyed each role and phase of her life. She feels each one has contributed to where she's at now, living her dream, doing what she's most passionate about, and fulfilling the adage, "Do what you love to do, and you'll never work a day in your life."

When not writing and working with other authors, Sherrie enjoys spending time with her family.